LIVE THE LIFE ABUNDANT

"I have come that they may have life, and that they may have it more abundantly."
—*John 10:10*

"The Spirit Himself bears witness with our spirit that we are children of God, and if children, then heirs—heirs of God and joint heirs with Christ, if indeed we suffer with Him, that we may also be glorified together."
—*Romans 8:16-17*

"Your faith has saved you. Go in peace."
—*Luke 7:50*

ISBN: 0-9762014-6-1
13 digit ISBN: 978-0-9762014-6-5

Published by L'Edge Press
A ministry of Upside Down Ministries, Inc.
PO Box 2567
Boone, NC 28607

The drawings in this book were
done by Shelley Latham.

Table of Contents

ACKNOWLEDGEMENTS

When I think about who I want to thank for their influence in writing this book, I start and finish with my God. The thought that I only exist because of His desire is incomprehensible. So, first and foremost, I acknowledge Elohim, my creator.

David and Betsi Treppel are my mom and dad. God used them to establish the foundation of my faith in my formative years.

I want to acknowledge Terri Buccarrelli, for her selflessness in giving me up for adoption at birth.

God has blessed me with my wife, whose intimate relationship with God is second to none. He has used her, more than anyone else, to help me grow.

There are many brothers and sisters in Christ that God has used to influence and encourage me.

There are also many Holy Spirit anointed preachers that God has used that I would like to acknowledge. The first are the two pastors that I have had in my adult life; Bruce Johnson and Ron Poythress. Ron has shown me so much of the true character of Christ.

There are also pastors that I know of that do not know me. But God knows us both and used them for my edification of the Word. TD Jakes, Billy Graham, Joyce Meyer, Kenneth and Gloria Copeland are but a few of the paradigm shifters in my growth.

In taking this book from my mind and heart to what you are holding and reading now I must truly give credit where credit is due. I am talking about those who took my raw, broken, fragmented sentences and brought them to a book. Andrea Quarracino dealt patiently with my ignorance and lack of writing skills and edited the book. Tom Willis condensed my original title to what it is now and helped greatly in shaping the prologue. I thank Jeff Hendley for the expertise and insight that he shared with me to get the book where it needed to be. And more importantly, I thank Jeff for being obedient to God, in making available a Christian publishing company that truly makes a priority of communicating the message of God.

PROLOGUE

When I was young, I had no doubt that I would grow up to play professional soccer or baseball. I wasn't alone. I shared this belief with many boys my age. As I got older and headed to college, I had every reason to believe that I would get a good job and glide up the ladder to a lofty, well-paying position with a big office overlooking the city. This reminds me of the television commercial with children saying that they want to grow up to be "a mid-level manager who takes a pay cut." Of course, no one aspires like that. We dream big. When we are young, both physically and spiritually, we embrace this empowerment to follow our dreams and aspirations. We so easily believe, with "the faith of a child," that we really can do what God says we can do. We believe that we have a strong voice, that we can make a difference. We dream and visualize the career we are going to have; the marriage, family, and home we are going to create. Indeed, we always envision ourselves at the top.

So, what happens? Life happens. Someone draws outside our lines and our utopia is ruined. As we get into the reality of responsibility, accountability, bills, and taxes, we find it becomes just enough to stay afloat. We deal with setbacks at work and disappointments in relationships, and vice versa. We deal with people who put us down and confirm our subconscious fear. Fear that we are limited in what we can achieve. We deal with a lot of negativity and cynicism, rejection and manipulation. We get burned by some of those rock solid friends. The trust we have in others and in ourselves turns to doubt and disbelief. Our hearts are hardened by these disappointments and rejections. It becomes difficult to try to help someone, for we are cynical to their motivations and intentions. In turn, our motivations and intentions turn away from obedience and love for God to apprehension and measured, calculated steps that insulate us from others due to fear. We make mistakes by acting out of feelings and emotions instead of by the discipline of God, mustering each day what we can do for ourselves just to get by. At times it feels like each day isn't about *living*, but *surviving*. We justify and rationalize that where we are is okay, and that we can be content with the hand life dealt us. We compromise and bury the desires of our hearts. Now, some of this might sound drastic. However, if you search inside yourself, you might see a little of this in your history, too. I have since learned that life does not have to work that way; that there can be much more to it than survival.

This is the story of how God opened my eyes to a paradigm shift in Him and in myself—as well as in others—that has propelled me to an energized life in Him. I was transformed, and He empowered me to an abundant life. This shift has changed my relationship with God, my wife, family, and friends. I have become clear about who I am, and whose I am. It is my hope and belief that you will find the principles I have learned, the principles contained in this story, capable of bringing about the same dramatic changes in you that I have experienced.

I learned that the most essential element, the foundation of a Christian walk, is the intimacy of a one-on-one relationship with God. From God through prayer, meditation, the living Word, and through spending time—lots of time—alone in silence with God, we grow, mature, and change. God has taught me through the life and teachings of His Son, Jesus, my Lord and Savior. I am learning what it means to come under the Lordship of Jesus, and am coming to more of an understanding of His saving grace. I would not have been able to grow using the methods detailed in this book without incorporating the grace and love of God through His Son Jesus Christ. It was through an intimate relationship with my Lord and Savior Jesus Christ that I was able to attain growth in spirit, body, and mind. Time after time Jesus went to be alone with His father, and so must we.

God has called us all to use our gifts for His glory. The first hurdle I faced was to accept and believe that I had gifts. The next step was to figure out what those gifts and talents were, and to seek how to use them for God. In this book, I will explain how I was able to discover the answers to those questions.

I have found that not only can God use me to bless others when I am a willing and able vessel, but that I am also being blessed. We find so much in scripture that encourages us to strive forward, emboldened by the Spirit of God that lives within. Jesus says that He has come to "give us life, abundant life." Through scripture God shows us that we are "heirs with Jesus" who has "overcome the world" *John 16:33*. We are told that, "He who is in us is greater than he who is of this world." God says that we are "empowered by His Spirit that resides in us… For indeed, the kingdom of God is within you." Paul tells the Philippians that, regardless of his circumstances, he "can do all things through Christ who strengthens me." *Philippians 4:13*.

What I soon came to realize is that the changes in me were physical, mental, and spiritual. These elements of our being must work interdependent of one another for us to grow completely as a child of God, and to actualize what He fully wants to do through us and for us. My pastor, Ron Poythress, who has had a substantial influence on me, pointed out that Jesus taught from a holistic perspective. Holistic is the overall interdependence of the sums with the focus on the whole. That is what makes us complete in mind, body and spirit—the total makeup of you. I began to understand better what I was striving to become in Christ: To be whole, to achieve Shalom. This became very important to me. God wants you whole in all aspects of your life—physically, emotionally, spiritually, mentally, and financially. In your mind, in your heart, and in your relationships; in all things pertaining to you. Not to want, and not to be lacking. "The Lord is my shepherd; I shall not want." *Psalm 23:1*.

This book is about how God enabled me to utilize scripture for physical, mental, and spiritual empowerment to an abundant life. The abundant life is the promise of Jesus in John 10:10 that is available to believers as we align our word, actions and faith with the Word of God. Through this abundant life, God has given me a profound purpose, focus, and direction that has enriched my relationship with God, my wife, my family and friends, and my business relationships. Through application of the scriptures, I was able to learn to work in concert with the Holy Spirit to bring me to Shalom; to bring together the interdependence of my mind, body, and spirit. The word shalom, or eirene, is a Hebrew word for peace. It is a peace that is complete in all aspects of health, welfare, and relationships. It is a soundness and contentment in mind, body and spirit. Jesus uses the word as a peace of tranquility, safety and prosperity in all that you are. It means to be whole, with nothing missing and nothing broken. It is a peace that transcends the natural world.

What follows is an account of how God led me to shalom, to an abundant life, using the principles that I will cover in this book.

Chapter 1: Paradigm shift

In 1987 I was a college freshman, and a wide receiver on the football team. Everyone was bigger, stronger, and faster than me. In the wide receiver position, there were many others in front of me on the depth chart. I spent my freshman year on the scout team offense. We were the offensive subs who would run the plays of the next opponent for the first string defense. Basically, we were meat. I would get crushed day in and day out. It was tough and I realized that if I was to keep playing, I was going to have to put on size and strength. After my freshman year I started working out and pigging out. I spent a lot of time in the weight room, but even more time in the cafeteria eating until I couldn't breathe.

The workouts I did were typical: bench presses, lat pulls, shoulder presses, tricep press downs, curls, and so forth. This was the same routine anyone did, whether a football player or a weightlifter. I grew up on the Jersey Shore, where looking good on the beach provided the motivation for working out. The focus was not on strengthening the interior, but on how the external appearance looked. We can fool ourselves into believing that the external image is most important, and I certainly did. The process of being a Christian is no different. It is easier to work on the appearance of practicing Christianity than making heart changes on the inside. Just as with weightlifting, being a Christian takes work on the inside that will eventually surface to the exterior for others to see. "They will know you by your fruit," said Jesus.

I got bigger and stronger, but I soon realized that it didn't matter how much lifting I did. I wasn't going to be able to displace one of the starters. Even more discouraging was the fact that I was competing against men of the same eligibility, so it was not as if I would be able to move up after they graduated. I decided that I would keep working out and doing the things that I knew to do, and I would always be a backup player. At least I wasn't going to quit. I would still have the camaraderie with "the guys," and a feeling of belonging.

Really, there is nothing wrong with being a team player and being regulated to the role of backup. It really was more than I could ask for. I had only played football one year beforehand, during my senior year in high school. I was a backup kicker who weighed 140 pounds the first week of my freshman year in college, and here I was trying to be a wide receiver. I had every reason to be content where I was. But then, we can rationalize and justify pretty much anything we decide to do. I saw a sign at a gym once that read, "Whether you think you can or think you can't, you're right." However, as I was to find out, you do a disservice to yourself and your Creator when you don't allow yourself the opportunity to realize your potential.

In sports, as in other arenas of life, the word "potential" is overused to the point of dilution. But that is exactly what we are given as a believer in Christ.

"Therefore, if anyone is in Christ, he is a new creation" *2 Corinthians 5:17*. We are given the power of the Spirit of God residing in us. As I stated earlier we are "joint heirs with Christ." What does that mean? The power of the Spirit that led Him on this Earth is fully given to us. God has bestowed gifts and talents in us "exceedingly abundantly above all that we ask or think" *Ephesians 3:20,* that will be manifest when we seek the desires of our hearts and grow in Christ. This potential exists deep in each of us. And just as I was content with being a backup on the football team, we at times resign ourselves to being backups on God's team.

I have since come to realize that there are no backups on God's team. On God's team, the body of Christ, each of us has been given different gifts and talents to be used by Him, through us, for His purposes. In 1 Corinthians 12, Paul speaks of the diversity of the body, and how we all represent different parts of the body. Some are parts that have more visible roles, but are not any more important than those that are less noticed. "But now God has set the members, each one of them, in the body just as He pleased." *1 Corinthians 12:18*. One of the points I will discuss later is the importance of doing all we can, where we are, with what we have.

That, though, is where I was after my first couple of years playing college football: content with playing the role of the backup.

My roommate and good friend, Pat Harmon, told me to follow him—to work out with him and trust him, and I would get my opportunity to play. What I was about to discover is that I wasn't close to being prepared to be out there on the football field during a game. We can get frustrated with God for not allowing us to have more, for not entrusting us to be used by Him on the field of life. God, the perfect parent, only gives us what He knows we can be responsible with. The more we grow in Christ, and learn, the more we realize we know less than we thought we knew. As I stated earlier, I was doing the same old weightlifting and running routine that I always did. Just as we get set in what we are comfortable with in "being a Christian," I was in my comfort zone. Well, Pat started to stretch that comfy zone I had set for myself. We started doing exercises and training that were geared towards what I needed to be a football player and not a "beach" player. We were doing power cleans, squats, and lunges, as well as other exercises with extreme intensity. Pat had us doing agility and quickness drills. These were not set up as training exercises; rather, we played creative competitive games. I was going where I had never been before, and I was certainly out of my comfort zone. I was getting what I needed, and not what I wanted. God does the same thing to us when we allow Him in.

I did not see improvements immediately, just pain and soreness. I was expecting fast results, believing that I would see myself getting physically bigger. This can be discouraging when we are set in the mindset of immediate returns, or instant gratification. The same thing often happens when building a relationship with God. He will work to change us by building a foundation first; substance over style. When God works on us and puts us through the process of making us to who He wants us to be, it can be discouraging if we expect quick change. For me it took a lot, and continues to take time, perseverance, persistence, and faith. We can allow ourselves to get so caught up in a culture of instant gratification that we must be reprogrammed to "not be conformed to this world, but be transformed by the renewing of your mind" *Romans 12:2*. When you study the scriptures and look at the processes that many went through (such as Joseph and Moses, and even Jesus), you see that God's work to build us up is not a quick evolution. The apostle Paul wrote that we must run the race: not a sprint, but a marathon.

It is very important that you study the Word and learn of God's ways. God's Word is truth. God said that His Word would never change, that "Heaven and earth will pass away, but My words will by no means pass away." *Matthew 24:35*. When you begin to read the Word, you begin to know the truth of who God says He is and who He says you are. It doesn't matter what someone says about his or her opinion of God, or how you feel about yourself, or how someone else perceives you. Knowing who you are in Christ will allow you to persevere through any feelings, emotions, circumstances and situations that you may be having difficulty with. God's Word in you will carry you through.

Over time, as I stuck with my workout, I did see change. I got bigger, stronger, and faster. However, I also looked at my limitations and obstacles. I was still going to be behind those two other guys on the team. Pat said to believe him, and that the opportunity would come. "And let us not grow weary while doing good, for in due season we shall reap if we do not lose heart." *Galatians 6:9*. Even as things were progressing, I found that taking my focus off the goal led me to feel distracted, and therefore discouraged. When Jesus walked on water, Peter came out of the boat and walked on water to meet Jesus. When Peter took his focus off of his Lord, he began to sink because he was aware of his limitations instead of being focused on the limitless One. When we seek God and put our focus on Him continually we will not fail if it is His will. "I can do all things through Christ who strengthens me." *Philippians 4:13*.

Jesus says that a little leaven could run through and ruin the whole batch. I needed to be aware that I was allowing this negativity to come into my mind, my consciousness. If you allow it to take up time, energy, and focus it will sap your drive, momentum, and resolve to persevere.

God puts in our lives, at the right time, someone who can help us through a specific hardship. A lot of the time we are so inwardly focused with self pity, with our anthill that we turned into a mountain, that we are not aware of the person God is using to give us an answer.

At this specific time in my life, God used Pat to show me the way. I had to believe Pat when he said to trust him that an opportunity would come. I needed to be prepared. I was preparing myself physically, but even more importantly, I was learning for life that the mind is very powerful and can determine how far you can go physically. It is said that most success in sports is mental, and this applies to all aspects of life as well. I began to learn about the power of the mind.

The summer before my junior year, Pat and I did some running at the Atlantic Highlands. We both lived at the Jersey Shore, so during the summer we would get together to work out. There was no better place than the Atlantic Highlands to push one's self physically. There were steep hills and roads to be run. I was about to discover I had to go to another level. One day we worked out, and then went for a run. It was the middle of a hot summer day. We went to an elementary school, put on our cleats, and did sprints up and down a steep inclined hill. When we finished, we were spent. However, we weren't quite done yet. Pat told me to put my sneakers on, we were going to run an uphill winding street. Did I mention that it was in the middle of the day, in the middle of the hot summer? We started up the hill. I had to run up the asphalt because of the incline; jogging wasn't going to get me anywhere. We began our ascent running side by side. Closing towards the end, Pat went up ahead of me. He got to the top. Meanwhile, my joints, muscles, and throat were burning. My chest was torched. My head was pounding and my legs were screaming for me to abort the mission. I slowed up and looked to see where Pat was. Physically, Pat was not that far away, at the top, urging me on. Mentally, though, he was as far away as one could be. I was disillusioned by my circumstance, and my feelings.

What is very important here, and what I am going to discuss at length later, is that we often make erroneous decisions due to mistaken perceptions. Our perceptions are our reality, but do not necessarily define "reality." I was allowing the physical feelings of my flesh to distort what was actually in front of me. I wasn't that far away from reaching my goal. Many times the reason we fail at something is not because of our external circumstances and obstacles, but because of our internal barriers. And most of these are self-imposed. This is where we can be distorted by our "perception of reality." If we take the focus off our end point, our goal, our means will overshadow our ends. I was going to make the wrong decision by quitting so close to reaching the top. This would create a mental effect far more lasting than the physical toll of running up the hill. Truly, not making it to the top of the hill would not make or break me physically in the determination of my playing time. But the confidence and resolve I would attain, or not attain, would.

I was going to make a poor decision based on what I thought, externally, was not possible (the top of the hill was too far away). This decision was going to be made externally (my body is failing physically, overheating). Both were not true. I was going to allow circumstance and situation to dictate my choice.

I looked up to Pat (of course, miles away in my perception) and told him I could not make it. I was about to slow down to a stop when I saw Pat put his hands on his knees and look down to me. He said, "How bad do you want it?"

Because I learned to look past obstacles and my own perception of my physical limits, I did start my last two years of college football. It gave me great confidence that has helped shape me into the man I am today. With focus and determination, we can achieve more than we think we can. I have this experience in the catalog of references that I pull up when I am in a difficult situation. I have learned that I can persevere through arduous circumstances. I have learned that I can do all things through Christ.

In 1994, I was engaged to be married and I rededicated myself to Jesus after years of drifting away. By His grace He pulled me back. I started to pray and began to read the Bible. I went to Sunday school, church, and evening services. I also got involved in Vacation Bible School. I was changing things in my life, but at the same time I wasn't. I was just being religious outwardly, which is easier than truly being a Christian on the inside. I wasn't making internal changes; only external, only what others saw. I thought that this is what it meant to be a Christian. I figured that I was doing well and that God was satisfied with me. "Every way of a man is right in his own eyes, but the Lord weighs the hearts." *Proverbs 21:2*. It was easier to do tangible things to look good than to make heart changes, which at that time I was not even aware I needed to make. I was in my comfort zone. I was doing the "church" things but I was not about to compromise the rest of my life. I didn't feel any reason to deny or withhold anything that I wanted or wanted to do. God was in "my" box. I called upon Him only when I needed Him. See, He was my savior but I had not yet opened the door and allowed Him to be my Lord. This is directly why I would become frustrated with aspects of my life that I wasn't satisfied with. I wanted to change my behavior, attitude, and level of faith. However, I always reacted in the same fleshly ways, depending on the circumstance or situation. I allowed my feelings and emotions to lead me to make the wrong decisions, say the wrong things, and show a lack of self-control at times. I always felt I was a go-getter, very positive and upbeat. I always said that I wouldn't let others get me down. But inevitably, something always did. I was a slave to my flesh. I did not have "God discipline." I started to talk to God about it, and my prayers and conversations got more frequent. I wanted my reactions, attitudes, and behavior to change. What I didn't realize was that I had to make internal changes before I could have favorable external results. God works from the inside out, and He was about to show me how He works. I was, not realizing it at the time, seeking. "Seek and you shall find, ask and it will be given to you, knock and the door will be opened." We must take action and do our part.

It was a Sunday in the fall of 1999. This Sunday, as most, we went to Sunday school and then church. We came home, and I went to visit a brother in Christ who was in the hospital. So, I was doing good. God must be really pleased with me, I thought. That evening I broke out my Bible and started reading with one eye on the clock. See, I was a big fan of the law drama *The Practice*. I was a loyal watcher of many television shows. The fictional world of Hollywood was my reality. The week before, *The Practice* had a part one of two episodes. This particular night at 9 o'clock, the second episode would air. Since the previous show, I had made a mental note that I had to see the conclusion. It wasn't something that occupied my mind all week, but I knew come Sunday at 9pm I would be there in front of the television watching. The closer the time came to 9pm, the more I would look up from the Bible (which I wasn't wholeheartedly paying attention to at this point). As nine approached, I went into prayer. I gave God some lip service about how grateful I was and how blessed I am, and how much I love Him and… 8:59. Amen. I was settling in. I had already strategically set the remote by my left hand to pick up, aim, fire.

As I picked up the remote I heard that inner voice from God. Now, we always want to hear from God when it is convenient for us. Many times we look to Him in desperation, calling out for Him to do something or say something. I have found that God comes calling when it isn't in our "convenience." I didn't need Him right now. I didn't have a decision to make, or an uncertainty ahead. There wasn't a setback, or an insurmountable obstacle or hurdle to be removed. Now is not the time, I thought. I have had this program scheduled in "my time" since 10pm the previous Sunday. But internally, God told me to put the remote down and spend more time with Him. You know it is God when you try to ignore the conviction and it gets louder and louder. I just about rebuked Him in the name of Jesus. I mean, come on, I went to Sunday school, church, even visited with a friend in the hospital! Once again, "Every way of a man is right in his own eyes, but the Lord weighs the hearts." *Proverbs 21:2.* Jesus says, "Seek first the kingdom of God and His righteousness" *Matthew 6:33.*

I held the remote in my hand, thumb ready to apply pressure to the on/off button. I wanted to be a Christian on my terms, around my schedule. I felt that I already did put God first. But, going first in the day to Sunday school and church only came first in my day from a chronological perspective. I was putting this television show first in my heart. I was going to learn that it wasn't about what I wanted to do for God, how or when. It's about being obedient to what He wants, when and how. This is summed up in a statement made by a Spanish friar and theologian named John of the Cross, some 500 years ago. "God desires even the least degree of obedience and submissiveness more than all those services you think of rendering Him." I was still an unaware infant Christian. I was under the presumption that as long as I was doing "Christ like" things, I was a "good" Christian. I was to learn that it is all about obedience to God's will, God's timing.

As the conviction got stronger, I was still fighting it. God, I will spend more time with you... at 10:00. As I look back, it seems ridiculous to struggle between God and a make-believe television show. However, I still am not always impervious to this temptation.

All I needed now was gravity to push my thumb onto the on/off button. As I stared at the blank TV screen, God asked, "How bad do you want it?"

I haven't watched *The Practice* since.

How badly did I want it? How did I get it? And what exactly is it? It is an abundant life fueled by the Holy Spirit, drawn by the will of God to fulfill the desires of my heart that God predisposed in me long ago. I had been so far removed from those "desires, goals, and dreams" I spoke about earlier; the desires we cultivate within when we are young both physically and spiritually. We have all the promise of abundant life from God in the scripture. So, how did I get from there to here? By working through frustration and struggle. How is it possible that who God says we are, and who we believe we are, go in opposite directions? One of the main reasons is mental conditioning.

We are conditioned by what we see, hear, and read. In Chapter 13 of Luke, Jesus compares the kingdom of God to leaven in bread. A very small amount permeates slowly but steadily throughout the dough, expanding and expanding. As we take in the spiritual food, we become empowered to strive forward to do God's will for us and through us. We are enabled to focus on His will and to be enriched and fulfilled, believing that we can excel and be victorious. As well, we also are not always alert to how powerful the mind is, and how we can be so conditioned by the world without being fully aware of it. In Chapter 12 of Luke, Jesus speaks about how easily we can be persuaded and deceived. He warned the disciples to be aware of the leaven of the Pharisees. In both illustrations Jesus shows how subtly both good and bad can take root in our conscious, as well as, and probably more dangerously, in our subconscious; and how they can both grow and change our stance, beliefs, and conviction. Whichever we feed more—our spirit or our worldly person—will dominate. It is very easy to be conditioned to allow things that are not of Christ into our minds. We are persuaded to tolerate and compromise to the demand of the world. The world tells us that we are just one cog in the chain of evolution, that life is only here on Earth, and that there is nothing else; that you are not bound by any moral truths. Therefore it is perfectly acceptable to look out for yourself, and do whatever feels good to you. Relax, live life to the fullest, and do not worry about consequences. There aren't any.

Well, I had allowed much of the world in to my life, and who I then was. I wasn't changing on the inside.

I was conditioned to watch television, and I had some three hours every night replete with worldly views, sex, and violence.

Why was I so conditioned? Why had I believed that I was limited, instead of believing what God said?

> Jesus says of His Spirit, "He will glorify Me, for He will take of what is Mine and declare it to you. All things the Father has are Mine. Therefore I said that He will take of Mine and declare it to you."
> —*John 16:14-15*

> "That in Me you may have peace."
> —*John 16:33*

> "We are His workmanship, created in Christ Jesus."
> —*Ephesians 2:10*

If all things are given to us from He who has all power and control, shouldn't I be striving farther and expecting more of myself? What holds me back?

I started to investigate myself. Sounds kind of weird, but I had to observe and pay attention to how I reacted to others, and to situations that arose in my life. How easily would I get discouraged? How easily would I allow myself to be manipulated or influenced?

In my investigating I also looked outside myself to observe what others had to say.

We are told no, don't, can't over 20,000 times by the time we are eighteen years old. I was getting ready to learn just how powerful mental conditioning is, and how pervasive in our world negative conditioning is. We can become so unconscious of how we spoon-feed ourselves frequent and heavy doses of negativity. We are not aware of how we feed off of negativity, or add to others' negativity. Jesus makes us aware of this in the passages I spoke of earlier when He said to "Beware of the leaven of the Pharisees" *Luke 12:1*. He is telling us that we are to be conscious of what we are listening to. For instance, if you listen to a certain talk show you are being fed one person's opinion. You might think that it is harmless, but you are reinforcing someone else's mindset that is permeating your process of belief. What am I listening to? Why am I listening? Do I need to be listening to it? This is what Jesus is telling them to be aware of. The truth, the word of God, is the only foundation that we should build our beliefs and habits upon. This enables us to have a clear and accurate picture of who we are to God.

Looking deeper into scripture, I read accounts of those God called who didn't believe they were up to task. They, too, had allowed negativity to dull themselves into believing they were less than who God called them to be. For example, there is Gideon: "And the Angel of the Lord appeared to him, and said to him, 'The Lord is with you, you mighty man of valor!' Then the Lord turned to him and said, 'Go in this might of yours, and you shall save Israel from the hand of the Midianites. Have I not sent you?' So he said to Him, 'Oh my Lord, how can I save Israel? Indeed my clan is the weakest in Manasseh, and I am the least in my father's house.'" *Judges 6:12,14-15*.

Gideon looked past the Lord his God and saw only his limitations. It doesn't matter what God said, Gideon put himself down. Somewhere on the road of life, the experiences he was exposed to set in motion his belief of who he was.

Jeremiah and Moses are other examples of those called by God. Jeremiah felt he was inadequate to be a prophet because of his young age. Moses believed he couldn't be used by God to talk to pharaoh because he wasn't a good speaker. What is so great about their stories is that we can see ourselves in their shortcomings, but praise God it is not about what we can or can't do; it is about who He is and what He can do.

Yes, indeed, we can look on these greats in the Bible and see them overcome their perceived inadequacies to allow the unlimited God to work through them. I began to realize that there was even hope for me.

The greatest example is found in our Lord and Savior Jesus. In the gospel of John, in the 8th chapter, we read of how Jesus was being fed negativity from the world. Just as others do to us, whether intentionally or unwittingly, the Pharisees were trying to poison Jesus with negativity by telling Him He wasn't who He knew He was. At times, they ridiculed Him. (A little leaven ruins the whole batch). I love what Jesus retorts—it is a powerful verse and speaks volumes. "I know where I came from and where I am going" *John 8:14.*

Jesus knows His mission, and He cannot be rattled. He is entirely sure of Himself. Well, He is so sure of us that He tells us we "can do all things through Christ who strengthens me," all things being His will for us. Jesus held the truth because He had a close relationship with His Father. You might say, well, that is easy; Jesus is God. He, though, was also fully man. He dealt with His natural senses as we do. He put His Father first in His life. He spent so much time with the Father, and was obedient because He trusted Him. We are to take the mind of Christ Jesus.

So, we first must realize and be conscious of the power of the mind. And, indeed, it is powerful. So powerful that Madison Avenue, the advertising mecca, will pay over a million dollars for a thirty-second commercial during the Super Bowl while you are getting up to use the bathroom or chat with friends, going to the kitchen for drinks and snacks, and only glancing at the television set. Why? Because it works! If it didn't, they sure wouldn't keep spending all that money. (A little leaven.) All that we take in, we are formulating into our mental storage. It is molding us into who we will become.

You might wonder, Where do I go from here? I have consumed a ton of negativity, and it is not something you just shake off. It is not something you will never be affected by again.

After I got back into the word and prayer that Sunday night I put the remote down in obedience, I went to bed. When I woke on Monday, I didn't have a revelation. I didn't have any spiritual experience that I was aware of. Now, years later, I realize that God did work on me that Sunday night. But at that time, I didn't feel any different. Come Monday night, I wanted to watch the Monday night lineup. I was conditioned for my senses to be stimulated by the made-up world of television. It was, each night, something to look forward to before going to bed, going to sleep, and then going to work again. The night before I had woken up to the fact that if I wanted to make changes in my life, my walk, my attitude, and my behavior, I was going to have to spend more time with God and the word. I was going to have to take away the junk on TV.

I couldn't just do nothing with the television off the whole night, though. Jesus speaks in Matthew, Chapter 12, about an unclean spirit leaving a man in search of another dwelling place and finding none. He decides to return to the man and finds him cleaned out and empty. The unclean spirit goes and gets seven other spirits more wicked them himself and they dwell within the man who now is in a worse state then before. This means that you can't run away from a problem without running to a solution. I couldn't just avoid the television. I had to not only subtract the hours upon hours of television I was accustomed to, but also learn to use that time constructively. Like a child who is bored he will always find mischief, if I didn't add something constructive I would eventually substitute television with another worldly vice. I needed to add something spiritual. It had to be something that was going to lead me to a closer relationship with God.

"He must increase, but I must decrease." *John 3:30*. If I increase my time in the word and in prayer it would directly result in a decrease in the world. More times then not we do this the wrong way. Thank God I was about to get it. Jesus says that, "Who loses his life for My sake will find it." *Matthew 10:39*. To lose our life, we assume that we must be giving it up. Our thought process is such that we associate sacrifice with pain. For example, some one who desires to lose weight and focuses on the sacrifice of not eating certain foods can easily become discouraged. Instead, they need to set their eyes on what they are going to gain in the stamina, strength, energy, and health that leads to vitality and empowerment. That is what Jesus is saying when He says He has an abundant life for us. For me to be able to give up the television, I had to approach that sacrifice from the standpoint of adding something new, rather than losing something.

I came up with "Subtraction by Addition." To effectively decrease an unbeneficial habit, I decided to concentrate on adding other beneficial activities. My focus would be on what I was doing, and not on what I was trying not to do. When we look at ourselves we tend to point out the things we would most like to change, instead of what we appreciate. Likewise, it is easy to focus on what we should not do, rather that enjoying what we are in the process of doing. Adding new habits would, in turn, minimize and delete bad habits.

I was not going to stop watching television directly. Instead, I would find other things to do.

1. Time with God.

At the beginning of the evening I always had the intention to get into the Word and prayer, to spend real quality time with God. But first, a little TV. Just a little. Check what's going on in the news, sports, movie channels, favorite sitcoms, the special on the History channel, and so on. Wow, three hours and a few yawns later, I am in the Word. In a few minutes I wake myself up to pray and go to sleep.

God must and should come first. "Seek first the Kingdom of God" *Matthew 6:33*. When I finally started my evenings with God, I didn't worry about what time it was. I wasn't close to becoming sleepy. I began to really get into the Word. My focus became lasting and strong. When we honor God, He honors us. I started to learn so much, it whet my appetite for more. I really began to study, pray, and meditate. I learned more about who God was, what He expected, and discovered more and more who I was in Christ. God, through the Holy Spirit, began to reveal gifts and talents that He had predisposed in me long before. I started to find out who I was, and who I wasn't. And now I wanted to seek how to use my gifts for His glory, for His will for me. Things got clearer, and I felt empowered to step forward and take action.

2. Time with my wife.

Marlies and I were married in 1995 and I always thought we had a great marriage, as did everyone looking at us from the outside. And we did have a good marriage. But just like everything else, we didn't realize how much better our marriage, our relationship, could be.

I love my wife, so I would do anything for her. Or would I? Consciously I did, of course; we all would make sacrifices for our loved ones. But I began to uncover how much I wouldn't do, albeit unconsciously. There were times when she wanted to discuss something, or she just wanted to talk, and I would be absorbed by the television. Rightly so, she would want my undivided attention. I would listen, or rather I would hear her, while my focus remained on what I was watching on television. Or if I wasn't watching television, we would talk only until one of my shows came on. I would stare at the television, occasionally glancing at her, nodding my head, never listening to what she had to say. She grew tired of me asking about something she had told me at least once the night before.

With the television off, without worrying about when the next show would be on that night, I would relax and sit back, and we would talk. I was able to communicate without having a covert strategy to get it over by 9 o'clock. Now, this change did not happen overnight, and it isn't completely at perfection. My wife would surely concur. However, our communication habits have gradually but consistently gotten better, and this has enriched our relationship. I realized that I had been more than just rude and disrespectful; I wasn't honoring Marlies, and therefore I was not honoring my God. Jesus says, "Husbands love your wives as He loves the Church." This needs to be first and foremost.

Marlies and I are so much more patient with each other, and have become a better husband and wife, better friends, and better parents to our three girls.

"Seek first the kingdom of God, and all His righteousness, and all else will follow."

When you put God first, He can work on you, then you can enrich and be used for your marriage, your family, your church family, and so on. This work started with me, and only after I started down God's path could my territory be increased.

3. Journaling.

"If you should say in your heart, 'These nations are greater than I; how can I dispossess them?'—you shall not be afraid of them, but you shall remember well what the Lord your God did to Pharaoh and to all Egypt: the great trials which your eyes saw, the signs and the wonders, the mighty hand and the outstretched arm, by which the Lord your God brought you out." *Deuteronomy 7:17-19.*

Our mind has cataloged thousands upon thousands of experiences into our log (mind; memory). These become our points of reference as precedent for other like-situations before us. As discussed earlier, we have been fed so much negativity that when a challenge arrives we regress in the same manner that we did in a similar situation before.

As I said, our perception is our reality, but not "reality." We start believing that we are less capable of achieving what is set before us.

I started to write the challenges I faced, and the uncertainties I had to deal with. Then I would follow up with what God did, and what He empowered me to do in these situations. I began a catalog of positive reinforcement.

When we are faced with a situation, circumstance, or challenge, our mind draws back a familiar reference that will give us confidence or discouragement. This is where we need to have positive references fresh in our minds. By writing them down, you can continue to revisit and build up your mental storage. Adding invigorating experiences will help subtract the discouraging negative thoughts, beliefs, and experiences. It allows you to have a clearer perspective closer to "reality."

We live in a time that is saturated with pessimism. We need all the help we can get. We must establish our climate and not defer to the world, dictating doom and gloom which keeps us from stepping out in faith, actualizing our heart desires, and being all God calls us to be. If we allow ourselves to be ruled by an established belief that "it" is for everyone else, and we look at our perceived limitations and see our obstacles as roadblocks, we will compromise and be content with less than who we are called to be.

Earlier I spoke of how Gideon saw only his shortcomings, and did not see all the good he was through God's eyes. Because of the power of the saturation of negativity, we become our own worst critics. We allow society to help us build discouragement and inferiority. The key word there is help us. We contribute the most to this mindset, therefore it isn't up to society to change; we must change, and take on a paradigm shift in how we perceive God in all His power and love for us.

In Paul's second epistle to Timothy, Paul encourages downtrodden Timothy to "remember the genuine faith in you," and tells him, "therefore I remind you to stir up the gift of God which is in you."

God has, from the beginning, set up reminders for His chosen people. For example, consider The Feasts. The Hebrew nation came together annually to observe, acknowledge, and remember the faithfulness, power, longsuffering, and love of God, and all that He has done. Regardless of whether they are wandering in the desert, crossing into the land of milk and honey, realizing the plan of God under David, or living in present day; It is a remembrance. A refreshment of purpose. No matter the circumstances, they remember that their God is an awesome God.

Write it down, revisit, and be refreshed. Your God is an awesome God.

Think of our Christian feasts, Christmas and Easter. He was born in the flesh and died that we may live and live abundantly. It is a promise made to us by Jesus.

4. Goals.

> "For I know the thoughts that I think
> toward you, says the Lord, thoughts of
> peace and not of evil, to give you a future
> and a hope."
> —*Jeremiah 29:11*

Seek God and He will reveal the desires of your heart.

When I started to seek Him without looking at the clock to see how much longer until one of my "make-believe" TV shows would be on, I was able to give my undivided attention to God. I was truly seeking Him.

Before my relationship with God was about quantity, then it became about quality. "Paradigm shift:" God searches the heart. My heart wasn't truly into it. God will honor you when you are genuinely honoring Him with the desire to seek and commune and know Him, instead of reading and praying as a routine in order to get God's favor.

His Spirit began to work within mine, and I started to seek and ask questions. "Ask, and it will be given to you; seek, and you will find; knock, and it will be opened to you." *Matthew 7:7.* God has plans for each one of us and has predisposed them in our hearts long ago.

What I found when I would be alone in silence with God, and sought His will in my life, was that over time the gifts and talents that were buried in me came to the surface. The passions and purposes of my life began to crystallize. I began to ask Him to show me how to go about doing His will. I would start talking it out, and praying to Him about what I felt He wanted. I was truly establishing a relationship with God in the process. In seeking the goals for my life, I came to God's ultimate purpose; for me to have an intimate personal relationship with Him, and to rely more and more on Him and not on my own feelings.

In becoming stronger in my faith in God's power, I began to set personal goals and business goals that seemed out of my league. In going deeper in my relationship with God, my "perception" of God changed dramatically. It was a real revelation, and an eye opening to who I was as well. When Jesus walked on water toward the disciples in the boat, as described in Chapter 14 of the gospel of Matthew, Peter jumped out and asked Jesus to command him to walk on water to prove Jesus' identity. When Peter looked ahead and focused on Jesus, he did what would seem, and is, outside of his boundaries. However, his focus was not on himself and his limitations, but on Jesus the limitless. He walked on water until he was distracted by the boisterous wind, and realized his own limitations and feelings. At this point, he began to sink. When we get right down to the goals, the desires, that God has put into our hearts, as outlandish as they may seem in our flesh, we find God's personal commandments to us to follow. See, when I put aside the many things I spent time on each day and began to seek His will, the distractions were placed in the background and God's will moved to the foreground.

When I speak of setting goals outside of my boundaries, I am speaking of just what you are reading; this book. I am, in no way, an author. This book project began in the fall of 2002. God lead me to put together all of my notes, and what I have learned in the last few years, in an organized manner. Then I asked, "What now?" I was then lead to share this testimony of abundant living by oral presentation. I have, for the last few years, taught a small Sunday school class, but I by no means felt comfortable being a public speaker on a subject that has only encompassed the last few years of my life. I told God that it seemed pretentious of me to get up and speak on abundant living, and how I have been lead to go about it. His reply: It isn't pretentious of Him, and it is about Him. All the goals and passions are to be used for His Glory. All I do should be to edify Him, not me. As John the Baptist says in John 3:30, "He must increase, but I must decrease."

In the last segment I spoke of journaling as a way of creating positive references. God reminded me of times at church, as well as other places in the last few years, when I spoke and received positive feedback. That helped change my outlook, and helped strengthen my belief that

I could do it. I have given this presentation quite a few times now, and feel very comfortable speaking to people about what I believe in, and I trust that God is with me when I am doing so.

He led me to write this book as well. The last attribute that I would ever claim is that of an author. Nevertheless, this is not my will, but His. I took the notes I had for my presentations and started to elaborate on each topic and method. To write at length really is loathsome to me. However, doing it the Holy Spirit really had me fresh and alive in filling up the pages.

I also talked to God about my business and what goals to set, products to add, and ways to approach different situations. He gave me visions of what and how the business would look like and how it would run. Over time, the vision came to actuality. The goals that I wrote for desired sales amounts seemed ridiculous. Then each month, each quarter, we surpassed. It was definitely all God because it was way out of "my boundaries," and physical and mental abilities.

What I am saying is that when I truly began to seek God's desires for me, my family, and business instead of seeking God to align with my wish list, I began to live the fully abundant life that He desired for me. The thing was that His wants for me were always so much better than what I sought on my own. A few years ago my wife and I decided it was time to find a new house. At this time we just had our second child, and we were ready to get more space. We found a realtor who was also a Christian, and who attended the same church as we did. She did her job well. She was finding just what we wanted, with everything we had on our wish list. We wanted a two-story house with a big fenced in back yard. It was time now to tell God to get on board. What happened next was one of those times when I knew I'd heard from God. Nope. Not what we wanted to hear. Maybe we needed to pray again, even longer and more sincerely. That would definitely do it. He would see how much we wanted this house. It was what we wanted. NO. In prayer, both my wife and I received the same word. It took the wind out of our sails, if briefly. We would be obedient. We talked to our realtor who, as I mentioned, walked with the Lord, understood. We were to cease thinking of moving for the time being. It lasted about 16 months, and then God spoke to both of us. He lead us to a piece of property, a builder and a house plan. Proverbs 3:5-6 never spoke so loud and clear to me, "Trust in the Lord with all your heart, and lean not on your own understanding; in all your ways acknowledge Him, and He shall direct your paths." We had to decrease our wants to allow His plan to increase in and through us. See, God knew that if we waited 16 months we were going to be able to afford more of a house, a brand new house. It was a house that we had built to specifications that we desired. God gave us more than we intended for ourselves. We love our home. How could we not, it was given to us from God. "Now to Him who is able to do exceedingly abundantly above all that we ask or think, according to the power that works in us, to Him be glory" *Ephesians 3:20-21*. Yes, I praise and thank my God.

Now, as I sought and prayed and set other goals, both personally and in business, I began to visualize in detail these plans coming to fruition. I focused on standing before people speaking. I visualized talking with book publishers. I visualize speaking to others about this book. I visualize many goals for my business in specific detail. I saw a new building with bigger offices and more products and employees. I would see specifics of daily work.

In establishing goals and uncovering the true passion for my life, I discovered what really energizes me. At times we get spread thin doing so many things, and we are not able to give our best to any of them. In this shift of who I am, I was able to gain clarity of purpose. Those things that were no longer a priority were treated as such. When you become conscious of who you are, you can be more focused on that which leads you to being more effective, efficient, decisive, and less compromising. Which all leads to being able to attain our goals. It is God's will.

Also, with a clear purpose of pursuit you will be able to concentrate on where you are going, instead of what you are going through when tough times and uncertainties inevitably come your way. When you can see your goals both on paper and in your mind, you are able to keep them in front of you despite distractions and surprises. Believe me, I am one of those who can get off track very easily. I can get up and leave my office to go to the front office and end up making detours and totally forget why I got out of my chair in the first place. For me, it was born out of a sense of necessity. God surely knows what I need.

I learned more about who I was and who God was when my relationship with God became just that, a relationship, compared to treating God as the great giver in the sky. As I started to see myself through God's eyes, I began to take charge in following through with the purposes God had for me. The interests I had, which peaked during these last few years, have led me to learn about those I could benefit from. I read books and listened to Christian leaders and teachers, as well as Christian business leaders and encouragers. I've occasionally read a book or listened to tapes on successful people, thinking that was my end goal: to be successful, which in my mind meant to be rich. However, as I had this shift in perception, my outlook totally changed. If I sought God and did His will, I would be successful. I would be fulfilled, have peace, and be blessed. Serving God by serving others in the capacity that God would have me became my definition of success. "But seek first the kingdom of God and His righteousness, and all these things shall be added to you." *Matthew 6:33*. "All these" is God taking care of you for what He knows you need.

How? How do we put aside the distractions and focus on becoming who God is calling us to be? To have what has been instilled in us by God to be brought to manifestation? In the next chapter, I will explore how God offers us the empowerment to realize His plan for us through scripture.

CHAPTER 2: EMPOWERING SCRIPTURE

I was beginning to realize that I needed to do things that were of God that were empowering and effective, which would in exchange eliminate inhibiting habits. I needed to find a way to strengthen my mind on a daily basis.

Reading scripture provided the means to strengthen my mind. I found scripture that spoke to me, and by reading it I felt lifted up, confident, and emboldened. Though I had learned of and became conscious of the power of the mind, and aware of subtle discouraging environments, I was still up against carnal and spiritual opposition. This opposition could be detrimental to my goal of striving forward towards the man of God I was called to be. In the sixth chapter of Ephesians, Paul speaks of being strong in the Lord and His mighty power. According to Paul, "we do not wrestle against flesh and blood, but against principalities, against powers, against the rulers of the darkness of this age, against spiritual hosts of wickedness in the heavenly places." *Ephesians 6:12*. We are to put on the "whole armor of God." Paul then details the definition of God's armor. When Jesus was tempted by Satan, Jesus only used one weapon: Scripture. There is power in the Word of God, and I started to become aware of this fact. The Word of God is the only truth, and what I see or feel is not true if it is not aligning with God's Word. What is true is not found through my efforts to be good, or by using will power. "'Not by might nor by power, but by My Spirit,' says the Lord of Hosts." *Zechariah 4:6.* We take in the words of the world and allow them to mold us. Where we live, the people we associate with, our experiences, our culture, our TV, our world. They shape our view of false truth. We need to be renewed back to the God of all time and what He says is absolute about you, me and everyone for yesterday, today and tomorrow.

I wrote down scripture that really spoke to me, and I would constantly—on a daily basis—feed the scripture to myself. These are some of the scripture verses that I found motivate me. I found scripture that gave me the confidence to remember that I have gifts and talents, and I can be disciplined to be obedient to use them where God would have me.

"Trust in the Lord with all your heart,
And lean not on your own understanding;
In all your ways acknowledge Him,
And He shall direct your paths."
—*Proverbs 3:5-6*

"And we know that all things work
together for good to those who love God,
to those who are the called according to
His purpose."
—*Romans 8:28*

"I am the vine, you are the branches. He who abides in Me, and I in him, bears much fruit."
—*John 15:5*

"Call to Me, and I will answer you, and show you great and mighty things, which you do not know."
—*Jeremiah 33:3*

"Therefore we do not lose heart. Even though our outward man is perishing, yet the inward man is being renewed day by day. For our light affliction, which is but for a moment, is working for us a far more exceeding and eternal weight of glory, while we do not look at the things which are seen, but at the things which are not seen. For the things which are seen are temporary, but the things which are not seen are eternal."
—*2 Corinthians 4:16-18*

"For God has not given us a spirit of fear, but of power and of love and of a sound mind."
—*2 Timothy 1:7*

"Eye has not seen, nor ear heard, nor have entered into the heart of man the things which God has prepared for those who love Him."
—*1 Corinthians 2:9*

"My grace is sufficient for you, for My strength is made perfect in weakness."
—*2 Corinthians 12:9*

"Blessed is the man who trusts in the
Lord, and whose hope is the Lord."
        —*Jeremiah 17:7*

"Now to Him who is able to do
exceedingly abundantly above all that
we ask or think, according to the power
that works in us, to Him be glory in the
church by Christ Jesus."
        —*Ephesians 3:20-21*

"Yet in all these things we are more than
conquerors through Him who loved us.
For I am persuaded that neither death nor
life, nor angels nor principalities nor
powers, nor things present nor things to
come, nor height nor depth, nor any other
created thing, shall be able to separate us
from the love of God which is in Christ
Jesus our Lord."
        —*Romans 8:37-39*

"I will be with you. I will not leave
you nor forsake you. Be strong and of
good courage"
        —*Joshua 1:5-6*

"Thus let all your enemies perish, O Lord!
But let those who love Him be like the
sun when it comes out in full strength."
        —*Judges 5:31*

"But God, who is rich in mercy, because
of His great love with which He loved us,
even when we were dead in trespasses,
made us alive together with Christ
(by grace you have been saved)"
        —Ephesians 2:4-5

"I can do all things through Christ who
strengthens me"
        —Philippians 4:13

"Be anxious for nothing, but in everything
by prayer and supplication, with thanksgiving,
let your requests be made known to God;
and the peace of God, which surpasses all
understanding, will guard your hearts and
minds through Christ Jesus."
        —Philippians 4:6-7

"Peace I leave with you, My peace I give
to you; not as the world gives do I give
to you. Let not your heart be troubled,
neither let it be afraid."
        —John 14:27

I wrote these and other scripture verses down in a
spiral index card notebook. I would read them to myself
and out loud. I would visualize myself striving successfully
in the areas of my life I wanted to improve and succeed
in. We have been inundated with so much from the
negative, callous world, and we need to interject our
own empowering messages. I needed to do this because,
though I would speak of myself as a confident and
self-assured individual, I was still apprehensive and not

totally sure of myself. I was probably unaware of a lot of this, but it was built into my subconscious. As I stated earlier with "subtraction by addition," the first battle to be won is the realization of the power of the mind. Jesus said to be aware, that "a little leaven ruins the whole batch."

I was now aware and was going to do something about it. I started with my power scripture. I read my scripture verses night and day. The psalmist says, "I will meditate on your word night and day." As I read them, I began to memorize these verses. Soon they came to the surface, and would be with me all day long. At this point, I can't turn them off if I wanted to. This is exactly what had happened with the influx of negative, detrimental influence that had permeated my mind for the first three decades of my life.

I would read my verses right before I went to bed. I felt it had more of an impact at the close of the day, as the last thing at night that I concentrated on. If the last thing you watch before bed is a scary movie, that movie will be embedded into your mental storage. Perhaps a nightmare would come from it. Or, think of the last song you listened to before turning off the radio. No matter how stupid or silly it is, you are singing it…and singing it. Well, here I was, working to keep empowering scripture on the brain instead.

The byproduct of adding positive elements to your awareness is the action of subtracting out those negative things that you are now aware of, those things keeping you from striving forward with confidence to do all that God calls you to do. At this point I was willing and able to discontinue habits that I didn't want, without the pain of direct sacrifice.

Chapter 3: Who God Says You Are

I felt that I had found something that was making a difference in my attitude about myself. Continually, on a daily basis, day and night, I read over my power scriptures and spoke them out loud and to myself.

However, I felt that I was still, at times, not always fully confident in who I was. And for that matter, who was I really? Who does God say that I am?

I looked up more scripture to see who God says I am as a believer in Christ Jesus as the Son of God.

> "Therefore, if anyone is in Christ, he is a
> new creation."
> —*2 Corinthians 5:17*

> "…an heir of God through Christ."
> —*Galatians 4:7*

> "…heirs according to the promise."
> —*Galatians 3:29*

"There is therefore now no condemnation
to those who are in Christ Jesus"
—*Romans 8:1*

"I will never leave you nor forsake you."
—*Hebrews 13:5*

"If God is for us, who can be against us?
Nor any other created thing, shall be able
to separate us from the love of God which
is in Christ Jesus our Lord."
—*Romans 8:31,39*

"But of Him you are in Christ Jesus,
who became for us wisdom from God—
and righteousness and sanctification
and redemption."
—*1 Corinthians 1:30*

Jesus says in John 16 that all the Father has given Him,
He gives to us. Jesus says that the Father Himself loves
you; and loves us even as we were sinners. If Jesus says that
God loves us, and the apostle Paul tells us in his epistle to
the Romans that we can never be separated from His love,
and we are also told that His love covers a multitude of
sins which He will remember no more, we should have no
problem believing that God loves us. So you would think,
and probably believe easily on the surface. But, do you
truly believe that, no matter what, God loves you? Well, of
course you do. God might hate the sin but He will always
love us. That is what the scripture says, and that is what we
have always been told to believe. And, indeed, it is true.

I had to ask that question myself. Do I believe that,
no matter what, God loves me? Does His love vary

depending on how far we slip, or if we are being willfully disobedient? I had to be truly honest with myself. I kept coming up with "yes," but why would I approach God differently depending on what I did or did not do? For some of us, when we go deeper with Christ, we find that we do not feel we are worthy or deserving of being loved by God. We might uncover our true feelings—that God's love is conditional—and we might realize that is how we love others as well. We consciously or subconsciously base our belief of who our Father is by how we believe our Father is.

Some of us were brought up to fear God's judgment. We were going to catch God's wrath and fury. From that, we may proceed like we are walking on eggshells; trying to step lightly and not slip up. Who wants to live like that? Would God really want me to live like that? Well, at times that is exactly what we might do, not so much to please Him but to avoid angering Him.

When I sin against God and go with my fleshly desires and wants, I feel guilt and feel that God must love me less. But we know that guilt is not of God. "Therefore, there is now no condemnation to those in Christ Jesus." Included in the well-over 20,000 times we hear no, can't, don't, and all of the negative power of the mind, is the pervasive thought of a judging God who gives His love only to those who truly deserve it.

Again, I go to the truth. The uncompromising word of God. All throughout the Psalms, the psalmist praises God that His "mercy endures forever" and that His mercy triumphs over His judgment.

Just as I was doing with everything else, I applied subtraction by addition. I would say out loud that "God loves Matt Treppel." The first time I heard someone suggest doing this as a motivational positive reinforcement technique, the word "corny" came to mind; even more so when it was recommended to say aloud that you love yourself. But I did it. I said it out loud. It took a couple dozen times of doing it before I could say it without laughing. And I am sure some people I know will laugh at me after reading this. Seriously, though, I was ingraining into my conscious and subconscious a fact that was true and I needed to believe this in order to be able to strive forward to be who God called me to be. You need to hear it continually, and on a daily basis. I was adding in a fact, and subtracting out the doubt and uncertainty that the world would help cement if allowed.

One of my favorite leaders and teachers is a man named Zig Ziglar, a very successful salesman who has helped many people to realize the gifts and abilities they have. This man of God tells a story of a boy who lives with his mom. Their house is in the valley, with mountains all around. One day the boy and his mom get in an argument, and the boy gets mad and storms out of the house. As he slams the door shut he yells back, "I hate you!" Well, with the acoustics of the landscape there was a delay, and then right back the boy heard, "I hate you!"

Uh-oh! The boy thought and hurried back inside. "Mom! There is boy outside who says that he hates me." Well, the mother, knowing it was his echo, told her son to go outside and tell the boy that he loves him. The boy went outside and did what his mother had told him. He yelled out, "I love you!" Sure enough, after the delay his echo came back, "I love you!"

We need to hear this from ourselves as well as from others. We need to love ourselves, for who we are. We reflect our interior disposition by how we treat others. Our fruits will reveal us.

"Jesus said to him, 'You shall love your
neighbor as yourself.'"
—*Matthew 22:39*

To love others, you must indeed love yourself first.
To love yourself, you must know and believe, without
a shadow of doubt, that God loves you. Jesus loves
you. "While we were still sinners, Christ died for us."
Romans 5:8.

To accurately determine who I was in Christ, I first
had to determine who God says He is. God gave Himself
many names for us to call on, and God is everything
we need at any given time. A book entitled *The Peace
and Power of Knowing God's Name* by Kay Arthur was
helpful, as was reading scripture on who God says He
is. I take great comfort in God's Word, particularly in
knowing that God does not change, and He is always
faithful even when we are not. The depths of His love
are immeasurable. Through the blood of Jesus, God
loves me unconditionally, and eternally. Relationships
may, at times, feel unfulfilling. We may feel that
certain needs are not being met. But as we come to grow
in our relationship with God, we come to realize that
He fulfills all.

Through His word I learned that His mercy is greater
than His judgment. I did not have to walk on eggshells.
God is my Father who loves me unconditionally and
lavishly, as Jesus illustrates in the parable of the prodigal
son in Luke 15:11-32. The story is really about the father
being prodigal. The father being God is the definition
of prodigal; recklessly wasteful, extravagant. Jesus shares
this parable with us to illustrate how much God wants to
bless, protect, and give to us even as we continue to fail,
ruin, abuse, neglect all that He offers. In the parable, the

youngest son demands and receives his inheritance and squanders it with not-so-godly living. After he figuratively and literally ends up in the mud pit, he goes back home with nothing. His father runs out to meet him while he is still a way off. He doesn't ask what he did, or where the money went. The father shows nothing but his love, and throws a party because his son is home. That is our Father. Foolishly in love with us, and blinded by both our righteousness and unrighteousness by the spilled blood of His one and only Son, Jesus. As I started to see my God for who He truly is (all-knowing, all-powerful, all-loving), I began to want to please Him—out of love, not out of law. And I owe it all to Jesus.

As I would spend time with God in solitude, I began to consider specifically who I was. When you know who you are, then you also know who you are not. You do not have to try to please everyone in every capacity. We will run ourselves ragged trying to wear too many hats. When you do this and you become exhausted mentally, spiritually, and physically, you know it is not from God. You need to focus on the will of God in your life instead of what everyone else wants for you, and even what you may think you want for yourself.

As I would talk to God, I would discover who I truly was and what fulfilled me as a person. I wrote down who I believed I was called to be in Christ, striving towards God's desires for me.

Just as I did with empowering scripture, I wrote down what identified who I was.

- God chaser
- Devoted and loving husband and father
- Healthy
- Servant

- Steward
- Leader
- Teacher
- Contributor
- Encourager
- Listener
- Honest
- Loving
- Friend
- God disciplined
- Other people focused
- Businessman

As God began to reveal to me these specific descriptions through His Spirit, I was aware that some were not characteristics of me just yet. Others, I most definitely needed to work on. At first it threw me off. Then, with insight from the Holy Spirit, I began to understand. This is how God saw me. These are the characteristics that He has predestined for me to grow and become. God sees the end from the beginning. For what already existed spiritually to manifest in the flesh, I had to do my part.

I wrote these specific descriptions down and said them out loud every night and each morning. I was solidifying my identity as a man of God. I was adding in my factual reality and subtracting my perception of who I thought I was, or who I thought I needed to be. (Just as I spoke of the examples of Gideon, Jeremiah and Moses.) As I spoke these words day after day and committed them to memory, I became more focused on improving on each of these descriptions. I was speaking them into existence. "Death and life are in the power of the tongue" *Proverbs 18:21*. Not only do you "walk by faith, not by sight." *2 Corinthians 5:7*, we also speak by faith and not by sight.

It was physically impossible for Abraham to become the father of many nations. He and Sarah were way too old to have their first child, and Sarah's womb was barren. He didn't believe the circumstances of what He saw. He believed in what he did not see. "Him whom he believed—God, who gives life to the dead and calls those things which do not exist as though they did; who, contrary to hope, in hope believed, so that he became the father of many nations, according to what was spoken. He did not waver at the promise of God through unbelief, but was strengthened in faith, giving glory to God." *Romans 4:17-18,20*. If we are faithful, we should speak what God says. It wasn't easy. It totally goes against worldly logic. But, just as worldly beliefs are habits, so is allowing the word of God be your belief even as it is opposite of the world. It is reestablishing who you are. "And do not be conformed to this world, but be transformed by the renewing of your mind" *Romans 12:2*. We already are conformed to this world, indeed we need transformation by the living word of God. I had to teach my eyes to see beyond what was in front of me. This is how we show we are trusting God regardless of what our eyes see. If God says He will meet all of your needs, stop confessing your lack. If He says He will never leave you, stop speaking that He isn't there. If He says you are righteous and holy, stop saying that you are worthless. Stop saying you are a failure if you mess up or make a mistake. He says you are victorious. Speak it! Stop speaking what you see and feel and start speaking of what God says.

When I first spoke to God and these descriptions came to light, I wasn't exactly being the best that I could in each aspect. As I became more conscious of being a "listener," I also became conscious of the fact that I wasn't always being a good listener. However, when it became part of who I believed I was, I would be more conscious of trying to be a listener. The same goes with pretty much all of the descriptions. I focused on being an encourager and a friend when someone I knew was down or discouraged. To be a good friend and encourager, I really needed to be a good listener. I found that each characteristic also improved the others. Just as mind, body, and spirit enhance each other "holistically," so does each identifying characteristic. Every gift and talent that was given to me by God improved the whole.

I will tell you, this knowledge becomes empowering. It just opens your eyes to more possibilities of an abundant life. What it has done for me is that I began to view God and myself differently. I began to see troubles as challenges, and challenges as opportunities. The opportunities are to serve God over my circumstances and not from underneath them. You will always have circumstances and situations that are trying. Jesus guarantees it, but tells us that by standing on His word, you will persevere. "Therefore whoever hears these sayings of Mine, and does them, I will liken him to a wise man who built his house on the rock: and the rain descended, the floods came, and the winds blew and beat on that house; and it did not fall, for it was founded on the rock. But everyone who hears these sayings of Mine, and does not do them, will be like a foolish man who built his house on the sand: and the rain descended, the floods came, and the winds blew and beat on that house; and it fell. And great was its fall." *Matthew 7:24-27.* You will notice that storms come to everyone, no one is excluded. Owning a business for ten years certainly has had its share of trying times. In general, the obstacles always are the same in one way or another. Financial issues, employee issues, product availability, and unsatisfied customers are some of the challenges that are going to be in front of me to deal with. Sometimes they can be serious problems that, in the past, could lead to anxiety and immobilization brought on by fear. I am empowered and emboldened to face these challenges. My faith and trust in my deliverer is so much more convincing. Using empowering scripture and words has lead me to believe that my God has an answer, solution and a means. "Be anxious for nothing, but in everything by prayer and supplication, with thanksgiving, let your requests be made known to God; and the peace of God, which surpasses all understanding, will guard your hearts and minds through Christ Jesus." *Philippians 4:6-7.*

Again, I say speak it! "For the word of God is living and powerful" *Hebrews 4:12.*

Each of us is given different gifts and talents from God to be used for God. Some words that might define you are probably different from the ones I wrote down and focus on.

For example:

- Empowered
- Invigorated
- Replenished
- Strong
- Enriched
- Influential
- Compassionate
- Mentor
- Emboldened
- Vibrant
- Nurturing
- Creative
- Forgiven

- Successful
- Humorous

What says God of you?

The One who knows you better than you know yourself? "Seek and you shall find." "Ask and you shall receive."

Say them out loud and say them often. For a laugh, say them while looking in the mirror.

"You are what you eat." Just as the saying goes, what we watch and what we hear is what we become. Are you feeding more of the world or the Word? Your flesh or your spirit? The apostle Paul tells us that we continually have an inward battle with us between our carnal man and our spirit man. Which one are you more equipping?

By putting God first and seeking His will, you can begin your search for who God is. Not your perceived notion, but who He really is; in doing so, you will uncover who you truly are. This world will pull you in too many directions, and divert your focus and concentration towards too many worldly distractions. These distractions could lead to distorted perceptions, which would keep you from taking grasp of who you are in Christ. In Christ we are told we "can do all things through Christ who strengthens me." *Philippians 4:13*. The problem is that the "things" that are God's will are different in our eyes, and we tend to try to do not what God is calling us to do, and/or that we are not equipped to do, because we haven't allowed God to work on and through us.

Adding empowering scripture and identification definitions to your "frontal" mind storage, as I like to call it, will strengthen your fortitude. You shall not waver, but will remain stable on the foundation of The Rock.

I added power words to my notebook of empowering scripture and identification. As with scripture, I found words that empowered and energized me. These words I linked to motivation.

- Empower
- Embrace
- Strive
- Captivate
- Transformed
- Fortitude
- Perseverance
- Excel
- Embolden
- Energize
- Achieve
- Utilize
- Enhance
- Enrich
- Invigorate
- Strength
- Vibrant
- Excellence
- Victorious

Each day, as I did with my verses and identity words, I went over my power words. I began to use these words in conversation, greetings, and quick interactions. As I began to use these words, I could feel my mindset change. Now in my "frontal mental storage" I began to feel confident in who I was. People will always try to knock you down, and many times we will believe that discouragement and compromise. Yes, as we have discussed, the power of the mind is very strong. But it also works to your advantage. I was feeding my mind empowering encouraging food, and it began to take over. It was subtracting out the negativity and self-doubt that can allow us to compromise and be less than God has called us to be.

Now, from doing this for so long, I feel that I am a different person when dealing with challenging situations. I look at challenges as opportunities. In the movie *Apollo 13*, the true story of a mission to the moon that not only had to be aborted but almost became a national catastrophic tragedy, there is to me a defining moment of seeing challenge as opportunity. Ed Harris's character is the head at mission control. While the engineers of NASA are fervently trying to figure out a way to bring the crew back to Earth safely, Ed Harris's boss says to another man in earshot, "This will be the worst disaster NASA has ever experienced." Ed Harris looked at him and replied confidently, "All due respect sir, I believe this will be our finest hour." How is your mind conditioned? Do you see a problem, or is it a challenge, an opportunity?"

As I stated earlier, our mind pulls up past experiences as references for all future encounters. Our reference is our perception, which will influence how we respond. With the continual feeding of empowering scripture, and with solidifying who I am, I have viewed challenges as opportunities to strive forward and be victorious. The man that Ed Harris played could not have just come to the belief that, despite incredible odds, they would attain success in bringing the men of Apollo 13 back alive unless he held a solid belief in himself. That belief has to be built. I continue to build that belief and stability daily through Christ Jesus, who makes all things possible. "With God all things are possible." *Matthew 19:26.*

Indeed, with God all things are possible. He has created our mental capacity to be buoyed by empowering thoughts. In 1975, Dr. John Hughes and Dr. Kosterlitz were studying neurological and spinal effects when they discovered endorphins. Endorphins, Endogenous Morphine, are naturally made morphine produced by the nervous system, which releases euphoria when the mind is excited positively. These anti-stress hormones relieve pain naturally. Endorphins are a precious gift from God. The more modern technology discovers medically about the body, the more we see an awesome design by God in the creation of the human race. There is more that has been learned about the human body that supports what scripture says is good for us. It is a topic we will discuss in further detail in a later chapter.

At this point I felt that I was laying down a good foundation for stability in who I was and how I was conducting myself as a man of God. God was building eternal strengths in me that were empowering me in who God was, and who I was in God. I was subtracting by addition. Now I started to look at how I could translate what God has done in me, in order to be a vessel He could use to work through me to serve others. How could I serve and contribute? Ultimately, all the work God does in you is to be used by God to touch others. It isn't about me. It is about Him. It is about Him using you as a willing and able vessel.

We are not merely influenced by others; we are also an influence on them, positive or negative, empowering or a hindrance.

I have found that there are two times of the day that are most important for us to prepare for dealing with the people that we spend the most time with and/or care about.

The two most important times of the day are traveling from home to work in the morning, and from leaving work to going home for the night.

1. From home to the parking lot at work.

The working of God in me isn't for me, but for Him. He wants to use us for His will, to be light and salt. Jesus says that you wouldn't take your light and cover it with a basket, but put it atop a hill to be a beacon. We are to be a beacon wherever we are. We must step outside into life—our sometimes chaotic always busy life. For me, it is very important that I prepare myself to be focused on Jesus and the embodiment of who I am when the day gets going. Some of our biggest characteristics can be formed in our work environment, good or bad, depending on whether we are being influential or being influenced.

I want to be seen as steady and dependable when situations at work get stormy. People put their belief and trust in you when you prove yourself to be stable.

In the 8th chapter of the gospel according to Matthew, starting with verse 23, a storm strikes over the lake the disciples and Jesus are crossing by boat. During it the disciples panicked, Jesus slept. They woke Him. Jesus calmly responded by rebuking the weather and the disciples for lack of faith. Could you imagine the perception of Jesus the disciples would have had if Jesus also panicked during the storm? Would we be so confident in Him during our storms? How about those you lead and/or work with? How would their perception of you be if you wavered at every unexpected shake up? Would they count on you, or confide in you?

As I drive to work, I go through all of the methods that I have discussed using scripture and empowering words.

I say them out loud. When I step out of my vehicle, I want to be submerged in Christ. No matter what comes flying my way, I want to be prepared to stand firm on the foundation of Christ, rather than allowing my feelings or emotions to illicit a hasty reaction. "Only let your conduct be worthy of the gospel of Christ" *Philippians 1:27.*

"So then, my beloved brethren, let every man be swift to hear, slow to speak, slow to wrath; for the wrath of man does not produce the righteousness of God." *James 1:19-20.*

We can talk about being a Christian, but do we walk the walk outside the walls of a church building? I've heard a man say that "the greatest cause of atheism today is Christians. We confess Christ with our lips, walk out the doors, and deny Him by our lifestyle. That is what an unbelieving world finds simply unbelievable." We are told to preach the gospel at all times, and if we must, use words. Most want to be Christ-like and walk the walk. We are so often blindsided, not prepared to deal with a person, situation, or circumstance that is unexpected.

I pray and talk to God about setting my thermostat. Why a thermostat? The other alternative is a thermometer. A thermometer reads the climate and mirrors it. If the room is cold, the thermometer reads that it is cold, and likewise if it is hot, it reads that it is hot. Basically, a thermometer has no control of its condition. We can so easily be persuaded to act in a certain way, or make a decision that we are doing only because we are allowing other people, situations and/or circumstances to dictate our words, actions and decisions.

This is reacting. Reacting is allowing the power of God to be taken from you and being a slave to our flesh, our feelings, and emotions. The apostle Paul talks about not being a slave to our flesh. We are no longer under the curse of Adam. We have been set free by the blood of Jesus. "If you abide in My word, you are My disciples indeed. And you shall know the truth, and the truth shall make you free." *John 8:31-32*. Jesus says the Word will make you free. That insinuates that we therefore, beforehand, are captive. It is so important to realize that being in the Word and meditating on the Word is the liberation we all need from the worldly ways, beliefs and thought processes our carnal man is entangled in. The Word changes us inside out. Having a close relationship with Him frees us in our trust to follow Him and not be dictated by everything around us. Regardless of the fact that Jesus went to the cross, His thermostat was set on God's will. While on the cross, Jesus asked God to forgive those who condemned Him and put Him to death, offering salvation to a criminal on the cross next to Him. Jesus kept to the setting of His thermostat: love. He so trusted the Father that He gave His life knowing the reward of obedience; sitting at the right hand of the throne. Understand, Jesus knew that He was going to be in glory. What Satan tried to do in the wilderness, after Jesus fasted for 40 days and nights, was to get Jesus to circumvent His suffering on the cross and go right to glory. This is what Satan tries to give us: the easy way out. We ourselves must have the cross as well as the empty tomb. "That I may know Him and the power of His resurrection, and the fellowship of His sufferings" *Philippians 3:10*. Regardless of what it brings us, we must keep our thermostat on His will for us to act like Christ.

We must set our personal thermostat. A thermostat is set to influence the environment around it. The thermostat doesn't change. We, by setting our thermostat, make a stand on the foundation of God and how He would have us behave—not reacting, but responding. Responding with the Word of God.

I set my thermostat, but what else? I had to live it out loud, speaking God's morals, values, and commandments. More importantly, I had to live and speak of God's compassion, mercy, grace, patience, forgiveness, and love. Freely has this been given to you, and freely you shall give. The more consistent and unwavering you are in being a thermostat, the more God is willing to use you as a vessel.

"For God has not given us a spirit of fear, but of power and of love and of a sound mind." *2 Timothy 1:7*. It starts with self-discipline; God discipline (other translations say "of a sound mind"). Not allowing others, situations, or circumstances to dictate your words, actions, and decisions. Stay disciplined to respond in the manner that God would have you respond.

When God finds you stable and disciplined, He will unleash the power that was predisposed in you by God. "For the eyes of the Lord run to and fro throughout the whole earth, to show Himself strong on behalf of those whose heart is loyal to Him." *2 Chronicles 16:9*. What will be manifest is the love of God. "All will know that you are My disciples, if you have love for one another." *John 13:35*. God is the perfect parent. He will not give you what you will not be responsible with. The Bishop T.D. Jakes has a great illustration of this in a story he tells in his teaching series "Heirs of the Promise." He speaks of a gold watch, and of how fine it was. It was a watch that he had purchased for his newborn son. He had his son's name engraved on it. T.D. put it up out of the boy's reach. He couldn't, for years and years, give the watch to his son, though his son was always near this gift, this prize, this valuable treasure. It was his and he was very close to it, but T.D., the father, did not entrust it to the boy until T.D. believed the boy would be responsible to have such a valuable gift. Same with God, sometimes we act like a four year old in our lack of discipline and obedience. The blessings are ours already, but will we be seen by God to be faithful to be good and faithful stewards of what He is to give us? Are you disciplined in being like Christ that others see it in you regardless of what's going on around you?

Ultimately, do those at work know that you are a Christian by your love, compassion, yielding, or patience? When I drive to work, I feel I need to be focused on setting that thermostat through scripture, prayer and my own little mantra. The people that I am going to be around all day are the ones who I will leave with an impression. What am I showing them? How am I acting when a group of them are acting differently? "Only let your conduct be worthy of the gospel of Christ" *Philippians 1:27*.

My drive from home to the parking lot at work in the morning is my time to set my thermostat for the day, to ensure that my day will be solid on the foundation of God. As I have been more consistent with being a thermostat instead of a thermometer, I have seen God working through me, for His purposes, in an awesome way. I have been blessed in being a servant for Him.

A few years ago a vendor for our company was in town for a delivery, and notified me that he had taken a transfer within the company and that this was the last time he would be down our way. He was set to leave and we said goodbye. He said that on his way out of town he was going to stop to eat dinner. I said that I would follow him there and eat dinner with him. He was the same age as I was, and he would talk about the nightlife in the town he lived in, and all he was doing. While I was following him to the restaurant I prayed that God would put someone in his path to present him the gospel, so that he could come to know Jesus as his Lord and Savior. Well, God came back and told me that I was going to speak to this man at dinner. I shook my head. Obviously, God didn't get it. Not here! I tried to ignore the voice inside. What happens? God gets louder. And there is not a max volume with God. I said to God that He would have to make the other guy ask something that would open an opportunity for me to witness—I was setting the conditions with God. We sat down to eat, and first thing, this man asks if my wife and I go to church. (Since when does God do what I say?) He said that he brought it up because he sees the scripture that we have on our desks, the Christian music on the radio in our office, and how we conduct ourselves. I used to live in the same town he was living in. I knew all the nightspots he talked about. I could have easily gotten swept into conversations of my past. I had to stand and not waver, and it made an impression. Because it did, because I didn't allow myself to be a thermometer, God found me usable. I do not know if my friend accepted Christ as his savior that night, and that was not His purpose. God's will was for me to be a witness of Christ, as I did. A seed was planted. God does the watering, and receives the increase. I will tell you this; I walked out of that restaurant blessed.

2. From work to home.

I had figured it out. At least I thought I did. However, I was going home and turning off my thermostat. It was as if that particular rule didn't apply to the most important people in my life: my family. When I walked in the door at home, I was relieved that the constant pressure of staying focused, not wavering, and serving customers was finished until the next day. I slipped easily into Matt mode. It was time to focus on what I wanted to do for the rest of the evening. I wasn't aware that I was so selfish and self-centered. I felt that I was making positive empowering strides during the day, and that these behaviors smoothly translated over at home. And since our home life, to me, was great, I didn't even concern myself with looking to work on myself for the betterment of my relationship with my wife and children. I would pray and thank God for showing me how to successfully implement methods using scripture and prayer to effectively stay at my thermostat, regardless of situations, and to "allow God" during the day. God started to let me know that there was still work to be done at home. That, yes, I was getting more consistent in responding and dealing with others and with situations in a God-like manner during the day, but I wasn't doing it at home.

I wasn't being the husband, father, and head of the household that I was called to be. Far from it. I allowed my wife to carry much of the burden for our children and the welfare of the household, and I wasn't taking the responsibility to be the man of God at home. It takes time, energy, and commitment that—truthfully—I didn't desire to use. So I unfairly allowed my wife to carry the burden of our household by herself, and I would get edgy when she became frustrated with having to handle so much on her own. I would tune out. Of course, that most certainly did not resolve any issue.

God calls the man to be the head of the household, to lead, serve, and love his wife and children. I had the mindset, like so many men do, that I was out there working all day and wanted to come home and relax and unwind. Well my wife, as so many others, works full time from the time she gets up in the morning to the time she goes to sleep some sixteen hours later. Not only was my behavior unfair, it also wasn't in the framework of how God says it should be. As God laid this on my heart and I became conscious of it, I began to fully realize that of all God wants to do through me, this was going to be a vital part of the changes I was going to have to make. And as I became aware of the dynamics of our household, this was a change I absolutely wanted to make.

Just as with any real change at the core, it would take work on a daily basis to bring it about. The first thing I did was to make a note to myself that I had to set my thermostat again when I left work to go home. On the ride home, I had to be conscious that I was going to enter a different environment. I was no longer the business owner who had to keep things moving and going in ten different directions at one time. I was now going home, where I was dad and husband; where I needed to put my focus on the children and on what I could do to help my wife. It wasn't about me coming in and setting the environment, but coming in and observing the environment to see how I could best serve my family. One of the biggest differences was that at work I didn't want to discuss issues at great length; I would get to the point, make a decision, and move on. At home, this needed to be much different. I needed to listen, and listen some more. There are things that need to be discussed thoroughly within a family. I had a small span of attention that was fine for the workplace, but certainly not at home.

I had to consciously put myself in a frame of mind to downshift, and basically be still. I would think about all the pressure that was on my wife, and I had to alleviate it. What was the best way that I found to do this? Stand still, make eye contact, and listen. I have a habit at work (that

I am slowly but surely working on improving) of walking away as I am finishing with one person and moving on to the next. A habit of trying to listen to someone as I will rudely be writing something down, thumbing through folders or looking for something. Stop and give your undivided attention to the person you are talking to. When someone does not give you direct attention when you are speaking, you realize how unimportant you, or what you wanted to communicate, will seem. You also will be less inclined to communicate with that person again, or as often. As I stated earlier, one of the most effective things I did to create better communication between me and my wife was to turn the noise off: television and radio. Stop and listen. When I do this, I feel that my wife feels that I am being respectful and caring, and is then eager to share more.

I make a careful attempt to get myself focused on my family as I make the transformation from work to home. For me, this is a very important time of the day.

Chapter Four: Clarity, Awareness, and Peripheral

I spoke last chapter about the importance of remaining steady and stable, regardless of what others say or do to you, situations that arise, or circumstances that you find yourself in. I call this setting your thermostat.

As I put these new scripture applications into practice, I realized that this was the key word in what I would have to do: Practice. Just as when you play a sport, play music, or perform, practice isn't like the real thing. When you practice, everything remains constant. When you get into the game, all constants do not stay the same. Things happen that you are not expecting, or are not prepared for. The action picks up pace, and the answers to how you should act or go about decision making will not be there in front of you on index cards. I was taking all of my scripture and words and embedding them into my consciousness, and it was making changes in me and through me. However, being consistent out in the world was tougher. In real life, you do not have time to confer with your notes to determine how you should act. Because of the daily work I was doing, I was making changes to who I was and it was showing in how I was presenting myself in my words and actions. So many times, though, situations would arise that I couldn't foresee, and I did not have ample opportunity to prepare myself. So I didn't respond, I reacted. I allowed myself to be lead by feelings, emotions, impulses, and other people instead of being centered on God and who I have been called to be.

> Jesus tells us to, "Watch and pray, lest you enter into temptation. The spirit indeed is willing, but the flesh is weak."
> —*Matthew 26:41*

> And the apostle Paul said, "Be sober, be vigilant; because your adversary the devil walks about like a roaring lion, seeking whom he may devour."
> —*1 Peter 5:8*

> Apostle John says, "Little children, let no one deceive you."
> —*1 John 3:7*

The one thing I ask from God every day is my "CAP." The acronym stands for Clarity, Awareness, and Peripheral.

So many times, after the fact, I found myself wondering why I'd said or done something during a conversation or interaction. Only when it was too late did I come to realize what the situation was really about. I would find myself defining a situation or conversation too quickly, and saying or doing something that may have been inappropriate, or not what was best for myself or for others. We are confronted with so many different opportunities to be Christ-like during the day, but so often I would be hasty. I asked God to give me the clarity to really observe and listen, and to have patience to get clarity before I respond. Clarity helps you to make wise decisions, and say (or refrain from saying) what is needed at that particular time. I always want to have the quick answer, the remedy.

My wife is a great example of someone who allows a situation come full circle before responding. She's like Colombo. Have you ever watched Colombo? Colombo was a TV detective who deliberately paced himself while collecting all the evidence. He didn't make any speculations. He left that up to the hot shots that always jumped on something as soon as any scenario materialized. Not Colombo. He will drive you mad as he slowly makes headway through the facts, and gets below the surface of what everyone else sees to get to what is really going on. He gets clarity through observing and listening. My wife forever listens, takes in what is said, and might not say anything until she has all the facts and/or feels God is leading her to a response. When you allow that, you are able to have a clearer picture of a situation, and can better add to the conversation.

Clarity is what we receive from God when we align our words and actions with the Holy Spirit. When we yield to the Spirit, we are allowing God to give us spiritual eyes. I have found that when I am patient and I allow the Holy Spirit to do His work through me, I gain a clearer true perspective.

More than a few times in Proverbs, as well as in other books of the Bible, we are told not to be hasty, but to hear all there is before making a comment or decision, not to rush to judgment. Just like Colombo who, unlike the other detectives running to an inaccurate conclusion, came to a clear conclusion in the end.

> "He who answers a matter before he hears it,
> It is folly and shame to him."
> —*Proverbs 18:13*

> "The first one to plead his cause seems right,
> Until his neighbor comes and examines him."
> —*Proverbs 18:17*

Having clarity also contributes to the processes you are in. God has us work through various processes—meaning, an experience that leads to something new, both in us and through us. God is always refining us in this way. It is very easy to get frustrated, and to allow emotions to carry over to how you deal with others. A lot of times we will go through a rough patch, a valley, and allow it to defeat us, unless we turn to God for what we need to learn from it. What is He teaching us? In the story of Joseph (*Genesis 37-50*), an overconfident boasting boy went through a process of near death, slavery, and false imprisonment to become a man who God found trustworthy, humble, thankful, and able to prepare a nation to feed all surrounding nations during a famine. He became a leader. And in the end, he realized that though others used the process for evil, God used it for good.

I have learned to step back from tough situations and seek clarity, to take an objective look at the process God had me in. This would allow me to have insight into what I was to learn from it. I have found myself going through gut wrenching situations day after day at work, which really began to bring me down. I finally stepped back, got still, and sought Him. For that time, the discernment I got from God was that I was learning to trust Him, just for that day. I was so used to planning weeks upon weeks in advance, looking at the broad picture and trusting God that in the end it would all come together. My trust began to grow when I started to trust Him each day, one day at a time, with every aspect of the day. I was able to see his hand at work more than when I would look back over weeks and months and just, after the fact, believe I had trusted Him. I went through that daily to learn to lean on Him for it all, every day. I didn't necessarily finish this process at that time, but I was able to persevere and strive forward knowing that God was doing this for my good and that, in the end, I would be a stronger and more trusting disciple. Think of the act of going through a process as going through time in school. Take medical school, for example. One goes through years of arduous, tedious, and lengthy studying to be able to be a qualified and competent doctor in the end.

There are times when we have roller coaster days. Up one day, and down the next. In those I find I am learning that no matter what, I have what I need in God to get through. "For I have learned in whatever state I am, to be content" *Philippians 4:11*.

> "My grace is sufficient for you, for My
> strength is made perfect in weakness."
> —*2 Corinthians 12:9*

The process is always in place to bring us closer to an understanding of God, faith, obedience, and a relationship with Him. Process builds foundation, which leads to stability.

Getting clarity allows you to achieve the result that God intends for you.

I find that seeking God about what I am going through empowers me to be confident that I am going to come through stronger, and more able.

Clarity and awareness go hand in hand. To ask for clarity, you must consciously become aware that you are in a situation or circumstance that you are not totally clear on. When we are not aware, we can go into self-destruct mode and allow ourselves to say and do things based on feelings and emotion. This can be detrimental to ourselves, and to others. So many times we speak without thinking, or offend without meaning to, simply because we do not fully understand. For example, imagine telling a friend that you will see them at their birthday party, only to find out later that their party was supposed to be a surprise. We just continue on, not grasping the affect we have, ignorantly doing and saying whatever comes to mind.

You can get an understanding of how this works by watching yourself on videotape. You might watch a tape of an event with family and friends, and see and hear yourself as you never have before. You might think to yourself, or say out loud, that you can't believe what you were saying on that tape. You might be surprised by your tone of voice, your body language, or the mannerisms you use. You see yourself as others see and hear you, and are then awakened to YOU.

Awareness comes from listening and observing. When we are running at the mouth, or are too busy being pitiful, we are not able to focus on others, or on our surroundings. I would very easily step into a conversation, and just let the words fly without discretion. One of the words I use for my empowering mantra is "leader." I feel that God has guided me to be a leader. To be an effective leader, others must trust and believe in you. You are more apt to follow someone when you feel they listen to you, and do not just spew at the mouth to be heard. You must respond in a manner that is respectfully willing to understand others. I wasn't like that. I was self-centered, and talked about whatever I felt needed to be said. Others might mold an unflattering image of a blabbermouth know-it-all, a person they are not going to have a great deal of confidence in. I had to learn to read the climate of the situation, to become aware. What I realized is that there are numerous opportunities to reveal your true capacity to grasp a situation, and numerous opportunities to demonstrate how you are able to handle yourself.

It would be interesting to come home at the end of the day and watch the videotape of your day. Let's go to the videotape! Let's see. Hmm. Here, in the morning, we are cut off pulling out of the subdivision, running late, getting caught behind a school bus. We are so consumed with being wronged and rushed that we miss the opportunity to smile and say good morning to the clerk behind the counter when we stop at the convenience store, the clerk who has been there all night. We don't pause to smile at her, so we do not notice the sadness in her eyes. We miss the chance to say something uplifting and encouraging. Because we are self-consumed internally, we do not have the awareness in this particular interaction for God to use us to touch the life of the convenience store clerk. We missed being a blessing, and receiving a blessing. Sadly, this could happen on many instances. And that is all it is: an instance. A brief encounter, passing, to be used by God.

Awareness really must come before clarity. To seek clarity you must first be aware, conscious of yourself in a given setting. I continue to say CAP out loud during the day, to become ever conscious that I am always in a position to show Christ through my words, actions and decisions. Jesus always gauged the environment he was in. He always sensed what others were thinking and construing about Him. He showed compassion and patience. He observed obedience and true sacrifice. Only He "observed" the widow giving the two mites into the temple offering. Because Jesus was God centered, other people focused, He was able to show compassion, feel the pain of others, understand and be understood. Jesus is our great example of clarity and awareness. He always knew what was truly going on.

We are called to be like Christ. I imagine that on many occasions I failed to show others the Christ in me due to my arrogance, propensity for running at the mouth, and lack of listening. Sadly, this was not done out of malice, but out of ignorance. This was the persona I was showing others; this is who people thought I was.

Be aware and have clarity before you jump in and put your foot in your mouth. Many times the Pharisees spoke hastily, only to have Jesus rebuke them with truth and accuracy that brought them to silence. When the people saw this, they were inclined to have more belief and confidence in Jesus than in the religious leaders.

Seeking clarity saved Nicodemus. Not having clarity cost Judas his soul.

In the first chapter of the Gospel of John, Nathaniel sought clarity about Jesus through a question. The presumption was that not much good came out of Nazareth. When Philip told Nathaniel to come and see Jesus, he questioned him with that presumption. Nathaniel, though, had an open mind and went to have a clear understanding of Jesus. And because he sought clarity, he came to believe and his soul saved. Jesus even paid him a compliment (*John 1:47*).

With clarity, you can achieve the result God intends for you. The result that God intends is God's will through you, to be used by God as a vessel. God! Please allow me to be "out" focused at each interaction, each conversation during the day so that I can seek the clarity in these situations to be used by you. To know what is truly going on, you must take the focus off of inward thought and open your eyes to those around you. Listen. Observe.

I have found, since I consistently sought and prayed for awareness and clarity, that God can use me, every so briefly, ever so subtly, to be a witness; to show love, compassion, or an interest. The blessing I receive always seems greater than the blessing being given. I can't tell you how much my eyes were opened when I shut my mouth and opened my ears. There are so many people who need to see and hear the love of Christ. Love is an action. Are you acting love? More times than not, we don't because we are not even aware of the opportunity. Seek and pray persistently and consistently for awareness and clarity, and then watch your eyes open to others.

I learned a lesson in awareness and clarity a few years ago. I was leading Sunday night service, and the discussion focused on being merciful and compassionate. I left that night and was hurrying home to watch a football game. At the last second, I stopped at the corner convenience store to pick up a copy of *Sports Illustrated*, which—for a soon to be obvious reason—had not arrived in my mailbox that particular week. As I pulled up and got out of my truck, a rugged man approached and asked me if I was headed toward the beach. (Just where I'd come from.) This guy seemed tough and looked as if he had seen his share of trouble. I glided into the store and threw a "no" to him over my shoulder. Well, it was the truth. I wasn't going in that direction. As I grabbed the magazine, the conviction of the Holy Spirit came upon me. How dare I teach mercy and compassion, and in the next moment be merciless and uncompassionate? I could rationalize one hundred reasons not to help this stranger out. He could be dangerous. I needed to get home, and it was getting late. Again, I wasn't headed in that direction. Hey, the priest and Levite had their excuses as well not to help a stranger on the side of the road. It doesn't matter. It is easy to speak of mercy and compassion, and it is easy to show to those you love. Jesus says that even the wicked do good deeds upon each other. Jesus showed mercy to all, from a prostitute to a convicted thief on the cross.

I walked out of that store and God did something for me that was incredibly awesome; a gift I was unworthy to have bestowed upon me. He let me see this man through His eyes. I looked at the man, and the first thing I saw was a boy. He was of age, but nonetheless, a child. He wasn't tough, he was worn, as if this merciless world had worn him out. His eyes gave away his pain and devastation. When I asked him where he needed to go, his lip quivered and in his tired voice he told me. As we walked to my truck, I saw that he had an obvious limp. On the way he told me he had physical disabilities and that he had been walking the last two hours trying to get back to his efficiency room before 10pm, which is when they locked the front door. We were about four miles away, and it was about 8:45. We first stopped at the grocery store to get him some food, for he had none. I dropped him off at his motel and gave him some cash, for he had none. I left there feeling ashamed, and blessed. In the years since, I have told this man of the love God has for him, and the good news of Jesus. I have prayed with him and for him. He lives day to day off of a disability check. I help him out here and there. To be honest, I can't imagine living the way he has to, and under the conditions that he does. I will tell you this, I feel unworthy to be in his presence, to call him my friend. He deserves so much more. What scares me is that there are many encounters and interactions that God doesn't so blatantly open my eyes to. There are those that I miss because I am not paying attention, am too wrapped up in myself. Now, I daily seek awareness and clarity that I may be used by God for His purposes.

The P in CAP stands for peripheral. I ask God to help me see beyond what is right in front of me; to be able to sense the environment, the climate of a situation, which leads to clarity. Things are not always what they seem. As I discussed earlier, inaccurate perceptions can lead to mistakes in words and decisions made, as well as actions we decide to take.

Paul tells the Ephesians (*Ephesians 5:15-17*) to "walk circumspectly, not as fools but as wise, redeeming the time, because the days are evil. Therefore do not be unwise, but understand what the will of the Lord is." What he is telling us is to be aware of what is going on around us. Observe, and be alert.

It is very easy to allow the day to work you, instead of having you work the day. Pause when you feel rushed, and allow God to work through you and to you. I find that I can get the whole picture of a situation by stepping back and observing.

When I first got into sales as a profession, I started by selling health club memberships. It was a high stress job. I was mostly dependent on commission on my sales for income, so it was imperative to me to close as many sales as I could. One particular time I was in my office with a prospect, going over all the obstacles that would keep him from joining. I would ask questions, and I had a come back to everything he said. He didn't have any reason not to join. He wanted to work out. We were close to where he lived. He said the payments were not a problem. We went down the line without sealing a commitment to go ahead and sign up. At this time I stepped out of my office, went to manager Dan, and asked him to come in. Hopefully, he could use his abilities and experience to bring the customer in. Dan sat in my seat, and I stood to his side and kept silent. Dan asked the man a few open-ended questions, and allowed him to talk. I watched as Dan sat quietly, listening to the man. And when the man was done talking, Dan continued to be quiet and gave the man his full, undivided attention. I was kind of puzzled. Then Dan leaned forward and asked the man if the money was a problem? The man hesitated, and then said that it was. Now I was really puzzled. The man had convincingly told me that money wasn't a problem. Dan worked out a payment plan, and the man joined the gym.

When I first went into Dan's office and gave him an overview of my sales presentation, I'd told him the gentleman said that money was not an issue. After our new member left, I went into Dan's office and asked him how in the world he knew to ask the man if it was a money situation when he said more than once that it wasn't? Dan said that the man had told him. Huh? When the prospect was talking, my manager said that he observed his body language and the tone of his voice. What he noticed was how his tone changed, and how he lost his eye contact when it came to the topic of money. He told me that in general it is hard for a man, compared to a woman, to admit that a purchasing obstacle is financially based. Dan said it was beyond what was on the surface, and that when we look at the peripheral we can come clear about what is the truth. He told me that successful selling is successful relationships. You must stop talking, start listening, and observe.

I learned a valuable lesson that day. It is so easy to go through the day missing the truth. Jesus was in the temple and observed the widow give her two mites as an offering. No one else saw her. They saw the beautiful robes of the rich and significant with their many coins, making noise in the offering and bringing attention to themselves. Jesus observed the woman and saw past the obvious to the truth. He had clarity on the situation. The widow gave more than the others because she gave all she had, and the others gave out of their plenty. Looking at this on the surface, our perspective would be that the others gave more, but this conclusion would have been inaccurate. Jesus had awareness and clarity, and knew the truth. Instead of commending the others, he commended the widow who was poor by man's inaccurate perspective but rich by Jesus' perfect clarity.

A great example of the CAP of Jesus is in Chapter 9 of the Gospel according to John. In the end of Chapter 8, Jesus escapes from a group trying to stone Him. As He fled and passed through the crowd, we are told in 9:1 that "He saw a man who was blind from birth." The last thing I would probably be doing is noticing anyone, if I was fleeing for my life. Even if I wasn't, it is easy to miss others when I am consumed with my own little world. Now, think about going through a crowd and noticing a blind person. It usually takes some time observing someone to realize they are blind. It isn't as obvious as someone in a wheel chair, or a person missing a body part. Jesus is our great example of awareness. He always was focused on His purpose of intimately touching lives. We are to be like Christ. We are to do as He did. We are to be aware of those around us, and be willing and able to be used by God as a vessel to reach others.

I found that to be effective with CAP, I had to be careful of the things I was saying and the conversations that I would find myself in.

> "Be sober, be vigilant; because your
> adversary the devil walks about like
> a roaring lion, seeking whom he
> may devour."
> —*1 Peter 5:8*

> "Little children, let no one deceive you."
> —*1 John 3:7*

> "Watch and pray, lest you enter into
> temptation. The spirit indeed is willing,
> but the flesh is weak."
> —*Matthew 26:41*

It is easy for us to not be conscious of the words we speak, of how we speak them and to whom. What you say and what you do have an effect on others, and therefore an effect on you. One of the most detrimental aspects of how we communicate with others is negativity. You might very well think that you do not speak negatively. However, the key word there is think. Let's again go to the videotape. As I said before, we would be amazed at how much negativity we engage in our conversations if we saw ourselves on tape for a day.

When I began to be attuned daily to CAP, I very much noticed casual negative talk in myself and in others. I was taken aback at how easily it was to step into the negative conversation of complete strangers. For instance, just after I began these exercises, I went into the bank on payday. The bank is pretty busy on Friday afternoon, everyone getting paychecks cashed and deposited, getting ready to go into the weekend. I was next in line when the guy in front of me handed his check to the teller. She didn't say a word or look up, until he mentioned that he wanted to cash what was left after what Uncle Sam took out. Well, the teller chimed in about how these fat cats get by without having to pay taxes as they get richer while the rest of us get robbed every Friday. The sarcasm and cynicism brought in the man to this guy's left. It was funny how comfortable he was, adding his thoughts, and how receptive the other gentleman and teller were to adding him to their conversation. Misery loves company, they say. The thing about it was, I caught myself about to say something negative when I went up to the teller as well. It is so natural for us to be that way. We've been conditioned to focus on what we don't have instead of being thankful for all that we do have. Realizing that this little episode doesn't in any way define who these people are, I think back to perception. If I walked into church on Sunday and one of the three people from the bank were up there preaching or teaching Sunday school, I believe that I would be naturally less inclined to put a lot of trust in what they are saying. Right, wrong, or indifferent— that is the way our perception of others works. How could I be negative with someone, and the next day try to teach them in Sunday school? I didn't do anything wrong, immoral, or unethical, but the way I represent myself outside in the world shows a lot about myself.

The same conversations are being held about the weather. It is either too cold, too hot, or raining miserably. We allow the weather to dictate what we say, and how we act. We allow this negativity to consume us. Can we honestly say that we are not motivated to do anything at work because it is raining outside? Would you give a flip about the rain outside if your baby were born that day? We learn to complain about anything and everything, and this kills our motivation. Negativity is poison to our spirit. We unintentionally become discouraged. We allow it to kill our initiative, to get past our feelings and emotions, and to detract from getting on with doing what God wants us to do.

One thing I try to do is to avoid and ignore the negative. And I certainly do not want to add to someone's doom and gloom. Just as it was so easy for that gentleman and the teller to add to the negativity of the man in the bank, it was that much easier for that man and the other two to have a negative outlook on the rest of the day, and adversely effect those they interact with. Do not add to someone's negativity. Interrupt it with something positive, encouraging, uplifting, complimentary. It in turn will sow life into you.

Let's go back to the videotape. We are in a hurry, and go into the convenience store where the cashier has been there all night, and had a bad night at that. When we are down, we feed that misery. We can very easily help that person stay there, or lead them deeper into despair or depression unwittingly by agreeing with them on something negative. The cashier might say something negative, like how it's a miserable rainy day. The usual response is to agree, and add to the conversation. However, if we have our CAP on, we realize that she has that sadness in her eyes and she is having a tough time. Interrupting someone's rut of negativity by finding something to say that is encouraging not only brings fresh air to their atmosphere, but it shows them that you care. They see you walk in that store again and they have a positive perception of you, which helps them to be positive. The next time you are in a busy line at a store and the cashier is having trouble getting everyone through, watch their body language change when you speak to them with encouragement with a positive tone.

We sometimes think that we need to be doing something so incredibly extraordinary to be working for God. It is the subtle things that usually aren't noticed by others that have the biggest impact on an individual. For a person who is "down" to have hope, usually the most impressionable act is one of simple kindness.

Do not add to negativity, as much as it seems inviting and welcome. People have it all day. Break it with something positive; an empowering word or compliment, encouragement. It will lift you up as well.

Earlier I spoke of how negativity (don't, can't, won't) stores in us mentally, and can lead to a poor outlook on ourselves and on others. One of the things we typically do is put ourselves down, especially when someone offers a compliment. Be conscious of what you say when someone compliments you. It is so easy to down play it, and say something unflattering or negative about our selves. Such as, "Got lucky I guess," "No big deal," "No problem," "No, I really did not do anything." Just as we talked earlier about the power of negative conditioning, this adds to it. It is okay to take a compliment and to give one. Two phrases come to mind: "Thank you" and "You're welcome."

Praying for and continually saying CAP to myself and aloud has been most effective for me on focusing on CAP consistently. I try to anticipate interactions and conversations during the day that God will provide for me to be constructive for His purposes. To be effective for God, we must take the focus off ourselves and put it on others.

CHAPTER FIVE: MIND, BODY, AND SPIRIT

The connection between the mind and the spirit is undeniable. When Paul writes in his Roman epistle that we should "not be conformed to this world, but be transformed by the renewing of your mind," (12:2) Paul is making the statement that our mind needs to be transformed from a worldly (physical) outlook to an unworldly (spiritual) outlook. This happens when we are able to discern that the processes we are going through are refining, cultivating, nurturing, and transforming us into God's likeness. Just as soreness seemed to be the only result of working out harder, I knew that sooner or later it had to have a positive affect. If you do indeed do today differently than you did yesterday, you should inevitably have different results. Allowing the process to take its time comes from trusting God. I trusted Him even though I didn't feel different after I didn't watch television that Sunday night. Growing in knowing who He is and His truths and promises will allow you to get through the purging process.

When we are stuck in the worldly thinking of the present, we can become very discouraged when we find ourselves facing uncertainties, obstacles and setbacks.

> "Therefore we do not lose heart. Even
> though our outward man is perishing, yet
> the inward man is being renewed day by
> day. For our light affliction, which is but
> for a moment, is working for us a far more
> exceeding and eternal weight of glory,
> while we do not look at the things which
> are seen, but at the things which are not
> seen. For the things which are seen are
> temporary, but the things which are not
> seen are eternal."
> —2 Corinthians 4:16-18

We must realize that we are continually being refined. I have learned to view challenges as opportunities; opportunities to serve and rise above the ordeals and situations of the day. Challenges offer the opportunity to pause and seek an understanding of what I am going through, and what steps to take to be empowered to overcome and grow in faith. God gives us spiritual markers so that when we overcome and become stronger, we see that God is faithful and that He has used those circumstances and situations to help us grow more stable and trustworthy. When we do not allow the emotions of the moment to control our words and actions, God finds us more able to be responsible as a vessel. I have come to realize more and more that I might not understand why I am going through a particular situation, but that God always sees me through. Maybe not in a way I would have chosen, but in a way that was best for me.

"Trust in the Lord with all your heart,
And lean not on your own understanding;
In all your ways acknowledge Him,
And He shall direct your paths."
                —*Proverbs 3:5-6*

A few years ago, I had this example of a spiritual marker in my life. My business was at a major financial crisis. At least, it felt "major." At this particular time, our business had slowed down considerably and there wasn't too much cash flow. We had a lot of debt, and a good amount of overdue payments. Our major supplier needed us to send a large amount of money in order for us to receive any more products. We were devastated, had no way of paying it, and didn't see how this bill would get paid without an increase in cash flow. This wouldn't happen until we got some more business, and to get more business, we needed to receive more products. It was a catch-22. One night I felt like my world was caving in, but I was trying to keep a brave face about it. My wife and I were sitting in bed reading. Of course I couldn't read, because I was consumed with our predicament. I put my Bible down and began to pray. I was giving God a lot of lip service. I was thanking Him for all He provides, including the faith I had in Him to see us through this. This is when I truly learned that God goes right to the heart. "Every way of a man is right in his own eyes, but the Lord weighs the hearts." *Proverbs 21:2*. As I was praying to God (or as I should say, lying to God), the presence of the Holy Spirit came over me and I was told to put my head down, chin to chest. Right above my head, I could feel the presence of God. In what could have lasted five seconds or five minutes (It was all I could bear), a great rush of power and light flew through me like a locomotive. It was scary, and all too real. Both the light and power stopped simultaneously, and then a voice in me and around me said, "This is just a glimpse of my power, do not doubt me again." And then it was gone. I say it was scary, but really, the experience was totally unbelievable. I opened my eyes and looked at my wife, who was reading her book just as she had been before I began to pray. She didn't notice as I looked at her in bewilderment, asking, "Did you not just see and feel that?"

When I looked back on this, I realized that I believed in God but did not necessarily believe that He would work supernaturally on my behalf. It is the difference in believing in God and believing God. Believing Him is believing what His Word says. His Word which is eternal. "Heaven and earth will pass away, but My words will by no means pass away." *Matthew 24:35*. I had to learn what the Word said. Commit it to memory and meditate on it until I believed. "And my God shall supply all your need according to His riches in glory by Christ Jesus." *Philippians 4:19*. I saw that our supplier was due a lot of money we didn't have, and we didn't have money coming in either. I leaned on my own logic, my own understanding, and didn't think there really was a way to get through this and survive. The thing is, I can't specifically tell you how we received all the money we needed within the next day or two. We had some unexpected deposits put down, and the rest is a blur. The end result is that God showed His power, faithfulness, and love. I do indeed put my trust in Him before myself. Sometimes we still find ourselves in tight financial positions, at times even deeper than before. Now I do not doubt that God is faithful to us when we seek to run our business and our lives to honor Him. It might be

His will to shut the door on our business some day, but I trust that He will open another door that He will have us follow to continue to serve Him. I began to realize that the business wasn't our provider, or our provision. It was God, and Him alone.

I see challenges as opportunities to learn about God, others, and myself. They are opportunities to serve and be empowered by God, and empowered by relationships. It is our relationship with God and with friends, family, co-workers, and others that can open us up to how strong and resilient God has made us. Through struggle, we can see how much other people care for us and would do for us. Challenges not only present us with a chance to push ourselves to the full potential of all of our personal attributes, but we also see that we can learn to rely on God and others. I have learned a lot about myself, God, and other people through these " short and momentary troubles," and have realized that indeed I have grown stronger in my faith in God, and in the strength He has given to me. Just as our mind, body, and spirit are at full strength when working interdependently, so are we when working interdependently with other people.

One aspect of the physical, spiritual, and mental connection is the focus on the physical body and how the health—or lack of health—of our bodies affects our mental and spiritual state. This, in turn, can enhance or diminish our ability to be an able vessel for God. This is often a sensitive subject. We live in a country so focused on physical appearances that talking about the mind/body connection is a sore point for many people. We, as a culture, have been brainwashed to believe whatever we are told by corporate America, which includes the pharmaceutical and medical industries. It isn't that all companies in the field necessarily value profit over your best interests, but the industry standpoint on healthcare does differ from that which is taught by the Word of God. I have learned from several people in the medical field who approach their teaching and practice of healthcare from a Biblical standpoint. I am by no means an expert, but I have spent time gathering facts and, in the last decade, have applied as much of this information as I can to the care of my physical body. The points I will illustrate are those that have had the most positive affect on me.

Because of the conversations I have had with people that focus on health care—and on food and exercise in particular—I felt it was important for me to share what I have learned on this subject. Based on my research, I came to the conclusion that many people have a hard time with health issues because they do not have enough accurate information to make healthy decisions.

> "I beseech you therefore, brethren, by the
> mercies of God, that you present your
> bodies a living sacrifice, holy, acceptable to
> God, which is your reasonable service."
> —*Romans 12:1*

> "Do you not know that you are the
> temple of God?"
> —*1 Corinthians 3:16*

In these two passages of scripture, Paul is speaking of the physical body as a spiritual temple. All that we see, hear, and read goes into that temple. However, fully believing in the interdependence of the mind, body, and spirit, you can see that all that goes into the temple influences the physical body as well. If we do not keep up our physical bodies, we can't expect to maintain maximum spiritual healthiness. In order for us to be mentally alert and keenly aware of our thoughts, words, and actions (CAP), we need to be physically energized and healthy. In order to do that, we need to eat foods that will nourish and strengthen our bodies, and we need to be invigorated by physical exercise. The more stamina and energy we have, and the less tired and sick we are, the more we are able to focus on serving God by serving others. I will discuss what the Word says to eat and not to eat, and how these foods play a part in your energy level and your body's ability to combat sickness and lethargy. Your body is the house of the Lord, and it was bought at a price. Physically, we should do all we can to keep a fit house for the Lord. It, too, is a witness for God.

Treat your spiritual body as if tomorrow it will be required. Treat your physical body as if you are going to live forever. I do not know who said this first, but I think these are good words to live by. You are never guaranteed your next breath, and your last breath will send you to eternity, either with God or absent from God. Therefore, first and foremost, it is most important to seek and find the Savior Jesus. Once you are saved, you want to serve God all the days of your life on Earth, therefore make sure you remain healthy and vibrant for long as you can.

First we are going to take a look at God's most incredible, complex, and beautiful creation: the human body. Then, using scripture as a guideline, we shall see how the food He tells us to eat strengthens our physical bodies. We will also look at what we have been told not to eat, and how those foods adversely affect our bodies. God has given us boundaries not to restrict or punish us, but because He knows what is healthiest for our well being in all facets of life. God made our bodies a certain way, and He lets us know the best way to uphold and strengthen the one and only physical body on earth we will ever have. Then we will look at how physical exercise blends in with the total fitness plan for the temple of God.

God has made us very self-sufficient to maintain our health, and for the body to heal itself. The brain alone is so vast in its ability that a comparable computer would take up the space of at least half the Empire State Building. Just thinking about all my thin little laptop can handle makes it incomprehensible to measure the ability of the brain. God is awesome, and He made us in His image. We are His likeness. However, we allow both our body and our spirit to be damaged through breaking of the laws of God.

Physically, the life of the human body is found in the blood. Jesus spilled His so that we may have eternal life. Our body is made up of approximately sixty-percent water. Eighty-percent is red blood cells. Red blood cells carry life to the vital organs that keep us alive. Blood cells carry the vitamins and minerals the body needs to feed itself. It can also carry degenerative products and diseases throughout our bodies. When we eat, the nutrients in the food penetrate the cell and the cell carries the nutrients throughout the body. The cells must be permeable to be penetrable.

"Lord, thank You for this food and I pray that you will bless it to the nourishment of our bodies. In Jesus' name we pray. Amen." Day in and day out, we pray that God will bless food that He never intended for our bodies. The Word is the Truth and the Truth will set you free. "You shall not tempt the Lord your God" (*Deuteronomy*

6:16). In general terms, when Jesus used this scripture to answer Satan in the desert, he was implying that God would save Him from something that was not good for Him. I know that the context of that scripture does not deal with the sort of food we eat, but protecting ourselves from what is bad for us does pertain to this discussion.

Let's take a look at what God says about what He has given to us to eat.

> "See, I have given you every herb that
> yields seed which is on the face of all the
> earth, and every tree whose fruit yields
> seed; to you it shall be for food."
> —*Genesis 1:29*

Here is our first introduction to boundaries, to instruction of what is good and right for our bodies.

Herbs that yield seeds and trees whose fruit yields seeds. Well, what are they? Webster's Dictionary defines an herb as "a plant with a fleshy stem, as distinguished from the woody tissue of shrubs and trees and that generally dies back at the end of each growing season." So, most vegetables and fruits are included in this category.

> "Among the animals, whatever divides the
> hoof, having cloven hooves and chewing
> the cud—that you may eat."
> —*Leviticus 11:3*

Sounds pretty gross, to use an oxymoron. What in the world is cud, you may ask? Cud is partly digested food that the animal chews and digests again. Cloven hooves are divided into two parts. God is very specific in what He deems as food for you. Remember that which we stated earlier: that the mind, body, and spirit are interdependent of each other. Each affects the other and when one is strengthened, the other two are also strengthened. This also works in a negative context—when one is weakened, all are also weakened.

I believe the reasons why we, in general, have such a hard time with food are threefold. First, as I stated earlier, many of us do not have enough accurate information to make correct choices about what is healthy for us. Secondly, many of us lack of knowledge of how the body works to maintain health, and how the different foods that we eat fit into the dynamics of the body. Thirdly, we tend to forget that our physical health, the foods we eat, and the exercise we do are not just matters of the flesh. To overcome the lack of discipline towards appropriate eating and exercise is a spiritual endeavor, more than a physical one. On the surface, that might seem far-fetched. But Paul reminds us that our fight is against an enemy not in flesh and blood, but in spirit. *Ephesians 6:12.* I believe this to be true concerning our personal battles with weight, health, energy, and vitality. We are a living testament for the Lord, and that includes this fleshly temple we temporarily have around our eternal soul.

Food in itself has become a god for many persons. It becomes a stronghold because we become obsessed with it, instead of keeping food on the mind only when our body tells us it needs nutrients. That is what our hunger pains are, a signal from our body that it needs nutrients for the continual function of living. But it does not need a super-sized fast food combo. That your body lacks nutrients is what your body is telling you when you have cravings. We assume the body needs food, any food, but this is not true. Your body is signaling to your brain that it needs nutrients. It isn't a lack of food. It is a lack of the vitamins and minerals the body depends on to function. When you eat healthy, you will see that your body tells you that it is full faster than if you were eating processed foods. Processed foods have had nutrients taken out and chemicals added so that packaged food can sit in a warehouse for a while, on the supermarket shelf for a week or two, and then in your pantry for a few weeks more. Natural food, the food that was intended for your body, does not last. Since the overwhelming majority of us do not do our own farming, we depend on others to prepare good tasting food that can sit on a shelf for a few weeks or more. This is processed food. Almost anything found in a box has been processed. Fast foods? Forget about it. The stories I have heard about what is contained in that burger and fries alone is just about enough to keep me away.

We have been inundated with the idea that we think about food not only when our body is hungry, but also because there are delicious foods waiting to be consumed. We have way too many food products to choose from, and we have an emotional attachment to the satisfaction a particular food will bring us. When we are going through a tough day, our minds will bring up foods that we desire, and we experience for a moment the taste and satisfaction that that food will bring us. Our mind will do the same thing if we are bored. Certain foods then become an obsession, something that we trust in; like a god. When we realize that we are called to be disciplined in this part of our lives, we can begin to be conscious of what we are putting into the one and only body we are ever going to have.

Again I refer you to CAP. Just as the day can get a way from us and we can be in such a hurry that we are not cognizant of our thoughts, words, or the opportunities

God lays out before us, the same can be said of the food we eat.

Our day can become a blur of one activity into another. Just as we allow thoughts and feelings into our mind during the day that can be detrimental, we falsely assume that snacking here and there has no affect on our physical bodies. What are most detrimental are the habits that we form. One such habit is a lack of discipline. A lack of self-control in one aspect of our lives often indicates a lack of self-control in other parts of our composition. When God's law isn't our center, we are breaking from the design of our body. Instead of contributing to our health, we are contributing to chaos. We are unsettling the balance and peace that we were designed for. I feel that it is important to be very conscious of the part food plays in our lives. I do not think you can underestimate the value to your overall growth when you are physically healthy and physically disciplined in God.

God intended food to be just that: food. God gave us boundaries in what to eat and what not to eat so that we might have healthy, robust bodies. We have made food an entity in itself. Instead of a need to fuel the body, food has become something we plan our day around. It is something we need to fight a "craving," or relieve stress. We have allowed creation to be a focus, instead of our creator.

Some may argue that the law has abolished the boundaries God established for what to eat and not to eat; that we no longer live under the law. We are under the new covenant. Just as there were those that were God's people, and those that were not. Exclusion has been transformed to inclusion through Christ. You can eat all foods, but not all foods are good for you. The apostle Paul states this in his first letter to the church of

Corinth. "All things are lawful for me, but all things are not helpful. All things are lawful for me, but I will not be brought under the power of any." *1 Corinthians 6:12*.

My point isn't to say there is a strict boundary of what you can or cannot eat, or what you should or shouldn't. I eat foods that would be in the cannot and should not category. It is that food cannot be a controller. You eat something sweet because you want to every once in a while, and not because you need it to escape or make you feel better. Anything in excess is unhealthy mentally as well as physically. The more natural food you eat, the more strengthened you will be mind, body and spirit.

Considering the span of medical nutritional advancement, what God told us was healthy thousands of years ago is just as true today as it was back then.

Alkaline vs. Acid: What does Ph stand for?

Ph is the measurement of alkaline to acid levels in your body. A good Ph balance is 7.36. Higher than that, your body is measuring more acid. Lower, and your body is measuring more alkaline. Culturally, we wrongly believe that we can take foods that we like and put the words "diet," "low fat," or "fat free" on the label, and thus we are eating healthy food. But diet foods are not produced naturally. I have yet to see a skinny cow. The healthiest foods for our body come forth from the soil, birds, and fish God created for us.

What has been added to foods to make them appear healthier, with less sugar or less fat, are chemicals that are not natural to the body. These foreign substances add acid to the body. Just as all nutrients are carried throughout the body through the blood, so are these detriments that can lead to sickness and loss of energy.

Over time, we subtly poison our body; our heart, liver, lungs, kidneys, and brain. Our body perpetually tries to maintain Ph balance. When we consume more acid, our body will compensate and use our alkaline reserves to match the acid. When our body does that, it stores the acid as fat. This is the body's way of protecting itself. When our body lacks the minerals it needs (such as calcium, potassium, magnesium, and iron), the body will protect itself by getting what it lacks from your bones to keep the blood Ph balance. This, over time, leads to osteoporosis.

Here are some examples of alkaline and acidic foods.

Clean (alkaline): Chicken, duck, pigeon, turkey, goat, lamb, geese.

Unclean (Acidic): Pork.

> "These you may eat of all that are in the
> water: whatever in the water has fins
> and scales, whether in the seas or in the
> rivers – that you may eat. But all in the
> seas or in the rivers that do not have fins
> and scales, all that move in the water or
> any living thing which is in the water,
> they are an abomination to you."
> —*Leviticus 11:9-10*

Unclean (Acidic) without fins and scales is all shellfish; shrimp, oysters, crab, etc.

Other highly acidic products we put into our body are alcohol, coffee, and soft drinks. As I stated before, many of our foods are filled with chemicals (preservatives) to give the food a longer shelf life. A lot of our foods are altered (processed) for our taste buds. The food is no longer near the natural condition that God intended for the body. Foods that are refined are nutrient deprived, and acidic.

Substitutes for sugars can be unhealthy and even thought of as dangerous for your body. Aspartame is a very common sugar-free sweetener that has been reported to lead to a lot of unhealthy psychological, neurological, and physical implications to the body. It has lead to headaches, migraines, dizziness, drowsiness, hyperactivity, severe depression, anxiety, insomnia, shortness of breath, and problems with both hearing and vision. It is an ingredient used in making paint thinner. It is used in most soft drinks, and it is highly concentrated in diet colas. One of the worst things we feed our bodies is diet soft drinks.

Other ingredients to keep away from include high fructose corn syrup, enriched white flour, and refined sugars.

It is best to eat more of meat from grass fed animals.

As far as portions go, super-sizing is super hard on your digestive system. Make a fist. Take a look at it. That is approximately the size of your stomach. That is how much you should eat about every three hours. It allows natural digestion without putting strain on the body parts that deal with digestion and waste. When your stomach has too much food to handle, it puts it aside. That extraneous food is not being stored as muscle.

Our food market is saturated with foods that are doing an incredible disservice to you. The world takes on a surface approach towards food, which includes natural farmed foods. Most farms now are corporate farms, not the smaller family-owned type of years gone by. The focus is all about mass production and quantity. The bottom line is money.

Being a business owner, I too can say that the bottom line is very important. But some things have been lost in the pursuit of quantity. One thing that has been done is the elimination of field alternating. After the harvest, fields should be allowed to restore their lost nutrients. This would allow for enriched crops the next season. Unfortunately, an unproductive field is an unprofitable field as well.

The more natural foods you can eat, the better off you are. However, I also suggest supplementing your food with a multi-vitamin. There are also wheat grass supplements available that contain concentrated natural vitamins, minerals, and antioxidants that allow your body to maximize its vitality.

The hardest part of trying to change your eating habits is convincing your taste buds. What a control on our lives that they have with our mind. When you are used to eating a lot of sugar your body doesn't want you to quit. You have set a foundation that will take time to be broken down and replaced. One of the ways that we did it at our house was eating the same type of foods, but with healthy ingredients. I wasn't too keen on this, but I have to give credit where credit is due: to my wife. She was concerned about our healthy eating habits, but more importantly, we wanted to create healthy eating habits for our children.

I love pancakes. A running joke throughout my family is the story of how I loved to go to IHOP and eat chocolate pancakes with chocolate chips, with a tall glass of chocolate milk. I would eat them as fast as I could because it wouldn't take very long for the stomachache to kick in. I loved the taste. It was way too rich and way too heavy, and therefore it provided a couple of hours of discomfort. Then my wife introduced wheat pancakes to the kids and me. Yuck, I thought at first. I remember just looking at her with a sarcastic smile. I, though, had to give it a shot. Knowing that my taste buds would change their reaction over time, I kept eating the wheat pancakes. Now I am used to them. We made the same changes with spaghetti and bread. We began to educate ourselves on healthy, natural eating. We became knowledgeable and disciplined. We did not diet. We were not restricting ourselves in what we ate, but in how we ate it. Once again, subtraction by addition is a healthier, longer-lasting way to approach food. Depriving your body of what it wants leads to the temptation to cave in. We battle in our mind with our body, and this is not healthy.

How does being an unhealthy eater have to do with being a vessel for God?

As I stated before and shared with you in two of my own stories, our physical, mental, and spiritual states are all interdependent. When we are tired and/or sick, we are less energetic. When we are like this, we are less patient with others. When we are tired, we are less alert. Emotional distress is directly connected with immune system distress. The purpose of your body is to store the Holy Spirit. This tent has to be able to carry out God's plan for you.

> "Then He came to the disciples and found them sleeping, and said to Peter, What! Could you not watch with Me one hour? Watch and pray, lest you enter into temptation. The spirit indeed is willing, but the flesh is weak."
> —*Matthew 26:40-41*

I grew up being heavily involved in sports, and am a big sports fan. Watching sports is a great example of the body and mind connection. When an offensive lineman, in football, gets physically exhausted, he will make more mental mistakes, such as jumping off sides. Quarterbacks will make bad choices in throwing the ball, and receivers may run the wrong route. Due to physical fatigue, they affect their mental condition. To be mentally tough in sports, you need to physically conditioned. Much is the same with life. To be highly spiritually conditioned, we are more effective when we are in a healthy physical state.

What we find is that people in general look for instant gratification outside of God's boundaries. God has given us parameters so that we can build a foundation of fortitude and stability. This takes time and process, which leads to delayed gratification.

We try quick fixes that are never God's desire for us. The pharmaceutical industry is a billion dollar business because we consume pills and medications to cure mental, psychological, and physical ills—mere band-aids to conceal a deeper hurt. God is the great physician who has given us the power to climb back to health from within.

Jordan Rubin recounts his story of renewed health from near death in a book titled *Patient Heal Thyself*. In college he was very athletic, fit, and healthy. Then Jordan began to get sick and started to lose weight, lose his hair. He grew chronically fatigued, and experienced arthritic pain. He lost a lot of weight and couldn't hold food down. This left him hospitalized. Jordan learned that he had Crohn's disease, a disease that involves the colon and bowel channel. He had inflammation of the large and small intestines. Not only was he very sick, but he was also embarrassed about it. He was unable to have control over his life. The disease controlled all that he did or didn't do. He was told that he would be bound to a lifetime of medication. Jordan sought cures throughout the medical field, but nothing seemed to work. What literally saved him was the Word of God. Jordan sought the principles of food from the Bible. He prayed for God's help, for he was helpless. God answered as He does so many times: It is in the Word. Jordan found that he had the answer; following order. The order of what foods were made for your body to take in, and which were not. Jordan learned to "Heal Thyself." He is now vibrantly healthy and is teaching others what he has found: that the Truth will set you free. It isn't an arrogant statement "Patient Heal Thyself." If you read his book your eyes will be opened to so much of how our body was made to heal from within.

We hold this capacity in all of us. I am not saying that all disease and illnesses are curable strictly by altering eating habits, but we have the power to undo so much damage through Christ. "I can do all things through Christ who strengthens me." *Philippians 4:13*. So many people die every year from diseases that could have been avoided by eating healthier.

God is the cure. With a person that goes to Alcoholics Anonymous, the first and foremost step to becoming healthy is to acknowledge that God, and Him alone, can set you free. Jesus had come to make that which was broken whole. If you have Jesus as your Savior, than He lives within and through you and makes all things possible. "All things are possible with God." It is by following His order, and being centered on Him, that we can strive to the optimum that He desires in us physically, spiritually and mentally.

We have freedom in Christ to choose. In our society, and especially here in America, we have so many choices. So much that is not good for our bodies, and not intended for our bodies.

An important aspect to successfully making the paradigm shift in how we see food is to properly identify and categorize it. As I learned to be aware of when I was eating, what I was eating, and how much I was eating, I began to become more disciplined. This became easier because I would be clear on what I was doing and why. Was I really hungry? Only eat when you are hungry. We can misidentify food for purposes other than it serves: nutrition, and energy for the body. Are you eating because you are bored? Is food a comforter to you at a tough time? Most of the time we eat without thinking. We might open a bag of chips and start eating, and eating, and eating. When becoming aware of how we use food, we can correctly identify what it is fulfilling in us at a particular point. As you get consistent, this thinking becomes part of your healthy lifestyle, and through this awareness and clarity you learn discipline. God gave you a spirit of a sound mind.

CHAPTER 6: EXERCISE

"Beloved, I pray that you may prosper in
all things and be in health, just as your
soul prospers."
—*3 John 2*

"I beseech you therefore, brethren, by the
mercies of God, that you present your
bodies a living sacrifice, holy, acceptable
to God, which is your reasonable service.
And do not be conformed to this world,
but be transformed by the renewing of
your mind, that you may prove what is
that good and acceptable and perfect will
of God."
—*Romans 12:1-2*

Treat your spiritual body as if tomorrow it will be
required. Treat your physical body as if you are going to
live forever.

Again, the physical, mental and spiritual aspects
of life are interdependent of one another. Each one's

strength fortifies the others, and exercise is an important contributor to physical health. To many it brings a visual of health and vitality; to others it is a monster, a dread. It doesn't have to be. Because we are over-saturated with information, commercials, and advertisements about the newest cutting edge gym, or home gym equipment, we become skeptical. When we try different programs and have little or no success, we can become discouraged from attempting to try again.

"It only works for everyone else."

"I don't have the time or money."

Once again, we are allowing distortions of truth to keep us from the truth. The truth is that when you have a paradigm shift in your perception of exercise, you can approach it with a healthy, realistic attitude. What happens, because of the overemphasis on appearance, is that people find wrong motivations for exercising. We feel that we have to exercise to lose weight, to look like the girl or guy in the magazine.

Here we need a paradigm shift in how we perceive ourselves, and in what comes to mind when we think of exercising. Start looking at exercise as a way to refresh and strengthen this incredible creation of God. When we see that we have become stewards of God's greatest works, we will be more conscientious in taking care of it.

My freshman year in college is when I started to work out seriously. I didn't have a choice. If I wanted to survive out there on the football team, I was going to have to get bigger and stronger. Over the course of five years I put on close to forty-five pounds of muscle. I had confidence in my physical body, and that led me to be outgoing socially. When my playing days were over, I kept working out because I liked how energized and strong

I was—and because I was frequently complimented. This carried over when I was working at a fitness club, where looks are everything. The atmosphere in the gym motivated me to work out even more intensely, and I began to eat very healthy. I ate a very high protein diet. I got bigger and stronger, and the compliments increased. So at this time I was as physically fit as I ever had been, but for the wrong reasons. I was able to attain physical satisfaction, but I wasn't doing it to have a healthy inside. I most certainly wasn't doing it for God. I was doing it for external appearance. I didn't enjoy all the foods I was eating, and I didn't like working out for as long as I did.

After I left the fitness club scene I wasn't able to maintain the frequency of my workouts or their intensity. Outside the fitness environment, I wasn't eating all those "health nut" foods anymore, and subsequently I lost some of my muscle mass. But my focus was moving from my outward appearance to my inside appearance. I was seeking living water. The "gym" life was one of instant gratification. I would have to continue working out at that level to remain where I was physically. Instead, I was searching for the eternal gratification that I was finding in Christ. As I have grown in Christ, I have come to realize that my physical body's health is very important. I work out now, but nowhere near as intensely as before. By and large I am a disciplined eater, though nothing like I was in those days from my past. However, I am much healthier now, for it is God's will that I keep this tent alive so that I can be a vessel for Christ. Yes, I do like the feeling of being energized and empowered. I also do it to please God. When you transform your mind to be healthy for God, and not because "I am fat and need to lose weight," you will enjoy the fruits of your labor. Losing weight is a byproduct of eating healthy and exercising, not the goal. When you're able to focus on exercise in that way the process will be easier, satisfying, and much more enjoyable.

By combining healthy eating with cardiovascular and resistance training, you do not have to spend a great deal of time exercising. Three days a week, less than an hour a day. However, if you do not have the time to exercise now, you won't be able to afford the consequences later. The apostle Paul says that physical exercise profits little. In comparison with the exercise of our spiritual body, yes, this is true. However, the little that we do can reap great rewards for our entire makeup mentally, physically, and spiritually.

Anytime you incorporate something into your life, you will voluntarily increase the time dedicated to it if it brings about positive results. When you learn how and why to eat healthy, combined with physical exercise, you will see quicker and longer lasting results.

When you are eating healthy food, the body can use more of what you are feeding it and will store less as fat. When you add cardiovascular and resistance training (weight training), you will simultaneously increase metabolism and burn fat.

So what does this mean? Metabolism is the process of food moving through your digestive system, being broken down, being used, and being discarded.

When your body has acid neutralized, having a healthy amount of alkaline due to healthy eating, it no longer needs to store fat as a precaution. Your body will use the fat (acid) to be neutralized by the alkaline. When you do resistance training, forcing a muscle to push or pull against weight (resistance), the muscle destroys muscle tissue and increases your metabolism permanently. Your body will require more protein to repair the muscle tissue. Fat is a supplier of protein. This is what is meant by "turning muscle into fat." You are burning fat at the same time you are increasing muscle.

Cardiovascular exercise is when you increase your rate of blood flow by increasing your heart rate. This is when you go for a walk, jog, bike ride, follow exercise tapes, etc. When you do this, your body is taking in oxygen that is carried through the blood. The blood goes to all the organs in the body. The more oxygen the organs get, the more vibrant and healthy they will be. The more oxygen you get to the brain, the more alert you will be. The more stamina and endurance you obtain, the more active you can be. God has given us gifts to use for His purposes. Not only must we be willing and able to use them spiritually, we must be able to use them physically.

Resistance training can reverse atrophy and retard osteoporosis. Atrophy is the decline of muscle strength and flexibility due to neglect. Osteoporosis is the decay of bones due to lack of nutrition.

Ten years ago, I was working as an assistant manager for a health and fitness club. One day the owner asked me to show a woman around, and to try to sell her a membership. Well, ninety-year old Dorothy crept in the front door with her walker. The first thing I did was wrongly prejudge her. (God didn't prejudge us, he gladly accepted us—a lesson in its own.) Dorothy seemed very frail physically, and seemed very apprehensive. Besides that, she needed the assistance of that walker to get around because she was so weak.

That first day, Dorothy rode a stationary bike for approximately seven seconds. I had to help her on and off the bike, and help her keep her balance. We tried a couple repetitions of arm curls using no weights. That was it for the day. I do not think she was too encouraged. I sure wasn't, and most certainly did not expect her to come back, let alone join. But after a few weeks of coming in three days a week, Dorothy did join the gym. In those first couple of weeks, she increased her time on the bike and started using 2 $\frac{1}{2}$ pound dumbbells for the weight lifting exercises we added to her workout. The eye opener for me was that a couple of weeks after starting, Dorothy walked using a cane. A few weeks after that, she came in without any assistance. She would get on that bike by herself and ride for a couple of minutes, and go grab her weights and do her resistance training. The biggest and best change, though, was her countenance, that big smile on her face. Being empowered physically gave Dorothy mental strength that gave her hope, vitality, and confidence. In a few short months she was not only a regular at the gym, but she also started swimming again for the first time in years.

We each make a decision about how we are going to live. We do have the choice to be healthy and strong. God created each of us uniquely. As the saying goes, "God don't make junk." We shouldn't treat ourselves as if He did.

You wouldn't, I hope, feed your baby a bottle of soda. Or, instead of baby food, give your infant chips and chocolate. If you owned a thoroughbred horse you most certainly would not give it beer, pizza, and a pack of smokes. When we buy dog food, we buy what is healthy for the dog and we give it fresh water. And yet, this is not what we do to our own bodies. We were made in the image of our creator, God Himself. If He doesn't make junk, don't feed it junk.

Earlier in Chapter 3 ("Who God says you are"), I state how effective it is to repeat the descriptive words of who I am, my power words and verses. It is important for me because in between, during the day, the world will try to bring me down. The negativity, sarcasm, setbacks, and disappointments will put doubt in your mind and can be discouraging. Every night and each morning, I refresh by reminder and it has an empowering affect on me. The same thing can be said for your physical body. At the end of the day you need to be refreshed, get your muscles back in order. When we wake up, we are awakening from hours of overcompensation. Our legs are rolling one way. One arm is wrapped around our back, as the other one is straight out to the side. Just as our spiritual and mind center's balance holds God at the center, we must get our muscles back in place. After we wake up all distorted muscularly, we get going to work or play and we will use one side of our body more than the other. So now we are really pulling ourselves out of balance. This leads to muscle aches and muscle pulls, which in turn lead to headaches and painful joints. The body moving out of balance causes some cases of migraines. We can do some good preventive maintenance if we take better care of our bodies.

Healing by Design is a very enlightening and insightful book by Dr. Scott Hannen, a board certified chiropractic physician and an ordained minister. It is a book in which Dr. Hannen merges medical facts with Biblical guidelines and shows that through better health choices, the body is made sufficiently by God to eliminate sicknesses and illnesses from AHD to chronic degenerative conditions, to trauma, to many type of diseases. As it says on the cover of his book, you are able to "unlock your body's potential to heal itself." The testimony to this is the story of Jordan Rubin in his book *Patient Heal Thyself*, which I spoke of earlier. *Healing by Design* is another book I highly recommend. Dr. Hannen states, "common sense alone would suggest there might be another approach to health than just 'taking a pill for every ill.'" Reading those words it does make sense. But we are so conditioned to do just that that we don't stop and question. We need a paradigm shift. It is time for us all to take back our bodies. Our family goes to a wellness chiropractor. The philosophy is preventative steps to keeping the body aligned to keep it working the way God intended it. This is different than most of the established medical field. The established medical field is more of a response to illness and sickness instead of one of prevention. At our chiropractor's office is a quote by Thomas Edison that is on the wall of the waiting room. It says, "The doctor of the future will give no medicine, but will interest his patients in the care of the human frame and in the cause and prevention of dis-ease." I was amazed to see how so many simple to serious illnesses and diseases are caused and/or enhanced by our body being out of alignment.

There is no doubt that we can be empowered to make Godly choices about our bodies that lead to life, life more abundant.

Conclusion

Jesus came to give us life, and life more abundantly. He has given us the recipe, the ingredients, and the tools. His living Word is the guide. However, He also gives us free will. It is up to us to show faith by action.

Imagine being given a membership to a first-rate health club with all the amenities. You have all the work out gear you need, with instructors to help you on all the machines. Having all this will not put you into shape until you take action, get into the gym, and work out. We must seek God and be in His Word so that we can continually learn about Him and, in the process, learn about ourselves; our true selves in Christ Jesus. We must take action to move the Spirit through us to maximize the light and salt we are called to be.

I love the word for peace, shalom. When I say the word or meditate on it, I have a vision of complete wholeness, a true meaning of peace. His is a complete peace that works not only in my physical body, but also in my mind and spirit. A peace not just within myself, but also within my marriage and my relationships. It has been and continues to be empowering to me. I like the opportunities I get to speak about my experiences because I am so excited about sharing and seeing these applications work in others. It is a great privilege God has given me to be used by Him to help someone else. God has continued to offer opportunities for me to share, because that is what we are to do in all that God gives us.

We are not to hold on to gifts and talents, but allow God to use us as vessels. All that Jesus had flowed through Him; He continually gave of His power, His love and compassion. He emptied Himself totally, which led Him to be totally broken that we may be whole. He came to "give us life, life abundant." It is our obligation to Him to strive forward and be empowered in mind, body, and spirit. We are not just "sinners saved by grace," we are the "heirs with Jesus." We are "holy" and "righteous." It is in me and it is in you. God shows no partiality. He gives freely to all.

God has given each and every one of us gifts. We must seek to have God reveal them to us, and to ask God what His purpose is for us to use them to serve others. We are not all called to be the same part of the body. We seek God, and He will show us our strengths. In the parable of the talents, it wasn't important to the Lord who started with what, for they all started with different amounts. It was more important to do their best with what they had. A quote from Benjamin Franklin that I keep in my conscious is to "do all you can with what you have, where you are."

I believe that God puts many people in our path to teach us. There are many people God has put in my life that have brought me to where I am now in character, integrity, and belief. What I wrote here was my experience, and hopefully there is one ingredient in here that you can add to the recipe of your life. I haven't always been able to follow these principles. I fall short and can get frustrated. I also notice that when I get back to these principles and disciplines, I have so much vitality in living an abundant life. And so can you.

As this book comes to a close, I want to make it very clear that what I have experienced and what I wrote of in this book is nothing without God. This is, by no means, a substitute for a personal relationship with God through His Son Jesus. All of what we think we can or ought to do is useless without our personal relationship with God; without talking to and listening to God throughout the day. He wants our devotion intimately with Him. He commands our praise to Him. Jesus is the foundation that anything in a Christian walk is built on. Through a personal relationship with Christ you can realize all that He has planned for you, and come to experience abundant life.

Practice Sessions

Helpful suggestions in applying the principles of this book.

Journaling

1. At least once a week. There is something that went on or that you felt that you can look back on for reference.

2. Write of circumstances/situations, feelings and emotions.

3. Be real. As if only you will ever be the one to read it.

4. Review past markers and put past dates of them that are relevant to you right now.

5. Write prayers.

6. Record how prayer was answered. How did you get through it? What did God do? How do you see His faithfulness?

PRACTICE SESSIONS

Helpful suggestions in applying the principles of this book.

Goal setting

1. Pray! Pray! Pray!

2. Look through God's unlimited vision. Allow goals to be over the top.

3. Speak it out loud as if already received.

4. Have both short and long term goals.

5. Have intangible goals.

6. Write the goals down.

7. Allow God to change directions as you go.

8. Write plan and take steps each day toward it.

9. Consistently keep in view. Look at them. Speak them.

Author's Bio

If observed, I hope that first and foremost, I would be recognized as a follower of Christ Jesus.

I grew up on the Jersey Shore in Ocean Township. On the five-year plan I graduated from William Paterson College where I played football. They also were generous enough to give me a BS degree in Accounting. My wife and I have lived in Wilmington, North Carolina for the last ten years. We have three beautiful daughters. We are blessed to own our own business. I am on staff with the Fellowship of Christian Athletes working with the coaches and athletes at the University of North Carolina at Wilmington.

I am blessed to be asked to speak at various churches and Christian organizations, high school and college athletic teams. The platform, of which all of my speaking engagements are based on, is living the abundant life.

For more copies of the book go to Amazon.com or email at mtreppel@charter.net.

www.ingramcontent.com/pod-product-compliance
Lightning Source LLC
La Vergne TN
LVHW011208080426
835508LV00007B/667